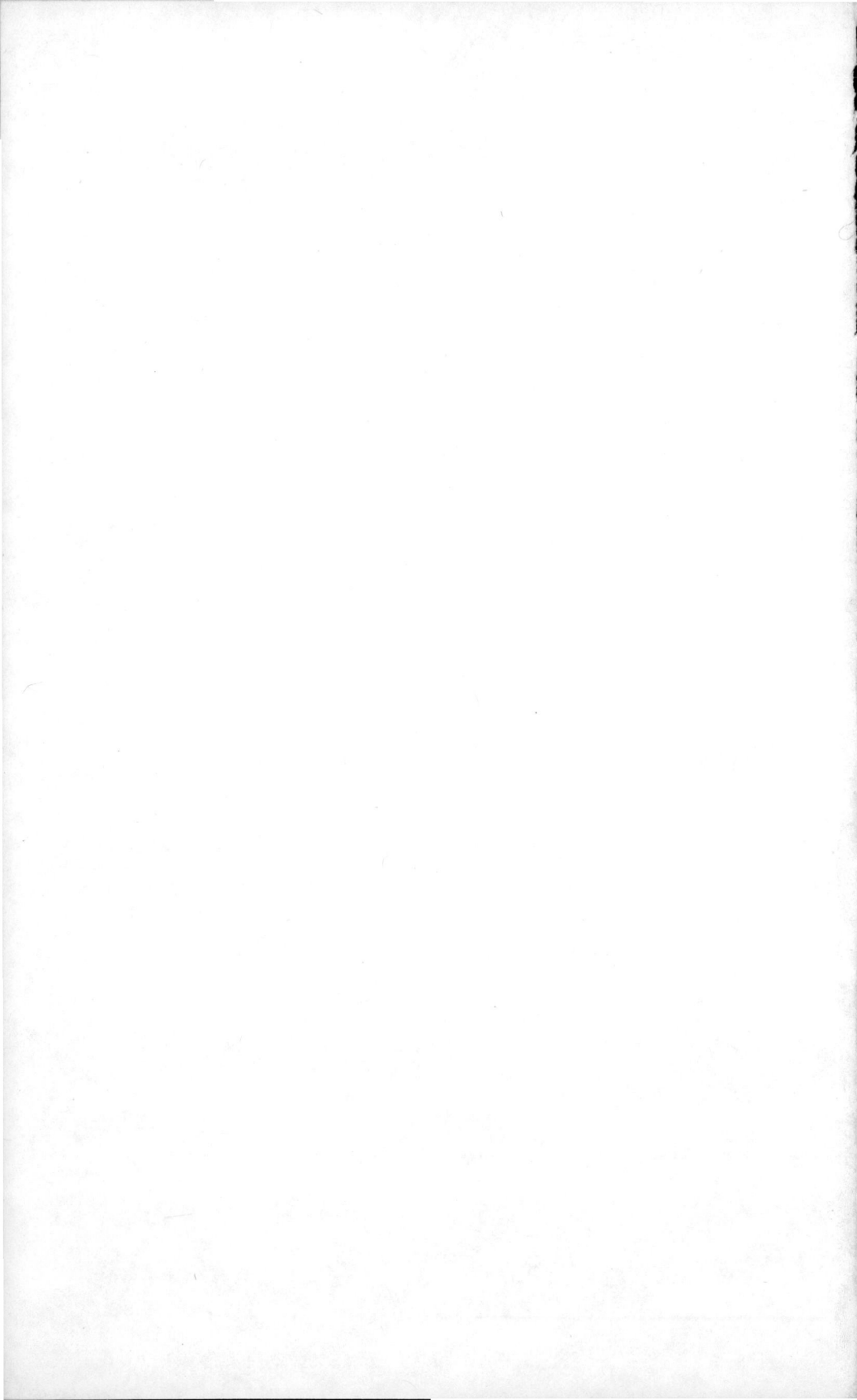

Strategy
FOR
Tomorrow

André Beaufre

Introduction by
RICHARD B. FOSTER

C R

Crane, Russak & Company, Inc.
NEW YORK

Originally published in France as
STRATEGIE POUR DEMAIN
Copyright © 1972 Librairie Plon

STRATEGY FOR TOMORROW

Published in the United States by
Crane, Russak & Company, Inc.
347 Madison Avenue, New York, N.Y. 10017

Copyright © 1974 Crane, Russak & Co., Inc.

ISBN 0-8448-0310-3

LC 73-94041

Printed in the United States of America

Stanford Research Institute is an independent nonprofit organization providing specialized research services under contract to business, industry, the U.S. government, and some foreign governments, particularly those in the developing nations. Since its foundation in 1946 in Menlo Park, California, the Institute's basic aims have been to enhance economic, political, and social development and to contribute through objective research to the peace and prosperity of mankind. The Strategic Studies Center of SRI was organized in 1954 by Richard B. Foster, Director. Based in Washington, D.C., the Center conducts multidisciplinary research on the crucial issues of foreign, defense, and international economic policy. With a client structure consisting of the key U.S. government agencies charged with responsibility in these areas, the Strategic Studies Center has long contributed to the ongoing dialogue in both the policymaking and research communities on the critical choices facing the United States, particularly in the field of national security. To make the timely findings of the Center's research available to a broader public, the Strategic Studies Center is publishing this series of books and monographs. The views expressed are those of the authors and do not necessarily reflect the position of the Center.

Contents

Foreword vii

Introduction ix

I. An Inventory of the Problems of Modern Warfare 1

II. The Level of Strategic Nuclear Dissuasion 13

III. The Level of Conventional Warfare............ 25

IV. The Level of Tactical Nuclear Deterrence........ 43

V. Reflections on the Navy 59

VI. General Conclusions 67

Annex: A Detailed Example of the Organization
of Territorial Militia 75

Index 91

Foreword

For the past twenty years, the Strategic Studies Center of the Stanford Research Institute has been conducting a unique multidisciplinary program of national security policy research and analysis. This program is directed toward the identification of alternative approaches to the critical problems which confront the United States in pursuance of its foreign, defense, and international economic policies; and in so doing, the Center's fundamental goal has been to assist its client agencies in the U.S. Government by presenting the results of this research and analysis in ways that will be of practical and timely value to the national decision making process. During this period of time, much of the Center's attention consequently has focused upon the political and military problems which confront NATO and the Western Alliance.

The complexity and magnitude of the problems facing the Alliance demand broadened communication and understanding among its members. The Strategic Studies Center has long sought to encourage and facilitate a nongovernmental dialogue on international security issues of common concern, particularly among research institutes charged with analyzing present policies in terms of future consequences. Its efforts have included the sponsorship of several recent symposia and colloquia, at which key European political-military participants and observers were afforded a forum in which to make their views known, and where exchanges of views between Americans and Europeans could take place. The Center has also inaugurated a series of publications whose purpose is to promote this crucial dialogue and to make its content and substance increasingly accessible to leadership within the Government and among the research and academic communities both in the United States and in the world at large.

One of the most important issues at stake in this dialogue is the search for strategic concepts and supporting force postures responsive to the requirements of the 1970s. Général d'Armées André Beaufre (French Army, Retired) has long been involved with both the formulation and implementation of new strategies for Western defense and security. In this study he examines the current status and the future directions of West European deterrence and defense, seeking answers to four of the most basic and vital questions of Western security policy today: (1) how to sustain extended deterrence in Europe in an age of superpower strategic parity; (2) how to adapt conventional force structures and tactics to changing conditions of offensive and defensive warfare and military technology; (3) how to define

vii

the deterrent and defensive roles of tactical nuclear weapons in Western security; and (4) what the implications of these factors will be for U.S. and West European national military force postures in the future.

Internationally recognized as a strategist and student of European political-military affairs, General Beaufre is eminently qualified to discuss these problems. A graduate of the French Military Academy at Saint Cyr, he has also attended l'Ecole de Sciences Politiques and l'Ecole de Guerre. His distinguished military career included command assignments in Europe and Africa during World War II, in Indochina in 1947, and in Egypt in 1956. General Beaufre concluded his active military service as Head of the French Delegation to the Permanent North Atlantic Treaty Group in Washington, D.C. Today General Beaufre is Director of the Institut Francais d'Etudes Strategiques, which he founded in Paris in 1962, and editor of its journal *Stratégie*. He is the author of numerous books and essays on military strategy and international affairs.

General Beaufre thinks and writes as a Frenchman. Nonetheless he carries on his labors within the broad context of European and Atlantic security. The subjects he addresses have significance not only for France alone, but also for the entire Western Alliance, if it is to cohere and prosper through the difficult times that lie ahead.

                                                    Richard B. Foster
                                                    Director, Strategic Studies Center

Introduction

The military problems of modern warfare are extremely complex, a fact which makes their correct formulation and efficient resolution very difficult. For years I have been convinced that an understanding of the evolution of current phenomena relating to warfare could only be obtained through the renewed and expanded study of strategy, which led me to construct a theory of what I called "total strategy." This constitutes the real framework of current confrontations, in which the existence of the use of military means represents only one factor. It is with this in mind that I wrote *l'Introduction à la Stratégie, Dissuasion et Stratégie, Stratégie de l'Action*, and *Bâtir l'Avenir*[1], while pursuing my research into loftier realms. The last of these books, *Bâtir l'Avenir*, repre-

---

[1] *Introduction to Strategy*, Armand Colin, Paris, 1963; *Deterrence and Strategy*, Armand Colin, Paris, 1964; *Strategy of Action*, Armand Colin, Paris, 1966; *Building the Future*, Calman Levy, Paris, 1967.

sented an attempt to establish a methodology for the study of the future wherein I encountered problems inherent in a philosophy of the future. Having set out to understand a specific problem, I ended up being confronted with the general problem of existence.

I would now like to return to the level of concrete problems faced by the military: problems such as the conceptualization of military forces, the genesis of weapons and the outlook for their use, and operational strategy. In other words, I wish to return to those problems faced by those who are in charge of national defense, i.e. of security in various countries. These unquestionably complex problems have a double nature: on the one hand, they are current and require each day practical decisions of considerable moment; on the other hand, they are related to hypothetical future situations. Perhaps never in the course of history has the future been more inscrutable, due to the lightning rapidity of technological evolution.

However, for various reasons, it is at present fashionable to scoff at the possibility of war as an historic phenomenon which has supposedly been rendered obsolete in the present day by the advanced state of our civilization and, consequently, to consider military problems as an old-fashioned facet of our traditional institutions. This notion, which has, however, been adopted only by a small segment of Western thought disoriented by primary sophisms, is far from being shared by the rising civilizations of the East and the Third World. The theory of "just wars," which strangely parallels that of Thomist philosophy, serves as a moral and intellectual crutch for the current armed conflicts which have taken place uninterruptedly since the end of the Second World War. Thus, it was important to start from the general concepts which I was able to glean from a study of the future and of total strategy in order to prove the current relevance of military problems. This is what I will attempt to do throughout this book in order to render true dimensions to modern conflicts in which military factors usually play a minor, but nevertheless significant, role.

This role, it must be recognized, has been profoundly altered. Modern minds shaped by the memory of the First and Second World Wars have an almost entirely outmoded conception of things military. This is because the conditions of war and peace—of action and deterrence—are no longer the same due to progress made in various realms, in particular that of weapons and intelligence. Under these conditions, the outlines of current thinking to which we are accustomed should be entirely revised, even though they often continue to inspire existing armed forces. Tactical organization and operational strategy are mired in obsolete formulae due to a lack of sufficient forethought to allow for development of a total awareness of the changes to be wrought. This is very dangerous.

It must be noted that the problem is extremely complex, for not only are non-military means of warfare being developed and perfected, but in the modern military domain scientific armaments, in the forefront of which can be found nuclear weapons, are introducing an element of confusion. The impact of deterrence, the heterogeneity of deterrence because of its different levels and the ever-present dialectic between deterrence and action render clear ideas hard to formulate.

To attempt to arrive at them, we at the French Institute of Strategic Studies have conducted a systematic study of the problems of operational military strategy over the last two years with the aim of formulating the most logical definitions possible of various categories of military forces, of defining the current state of deterrence and of reviewing the essential factors of battle with modern weapons. This study led to certain partial conclusions, often very interesting but the elaboration and justification of which could not be treated separately because of the interdependence of the various issues.

Finally, after several more or less successful attempts, it seemed to me more useful and convincing to write an overall work which would take up the explanation of the various problems from the outset and which would treat each as thoroughly as possible without any special effort at conciseness and especially without any concessions to current preconceived notions. As such, this book is a sort of overview of a number of problems on which there is a dearth of recent theoretical literature. Furthermore, even when certain ideas seemed revolutionary to me, but rich in perspectives, I did not hesitate to present them. This is the case particularly for the annex on "A detailed example of the organization of territorial militia" which, without straying from the subject, offers proof that new formulae are conceivable, for it is obviously necessary in certain fields to be able to transcend the boundaries of tradition. From thence come some conclusions which sometimes do not conform completely to present concepts; thence also come quite a number of repetitions for which I apologize, in order to present all necessary justifications for each case.

It is possible, and even likely, that these conclusions will be heatedly discussed, and even sometimes rejected. This is a classical process in the march towards truth. I personally am of the opinion that, taking into account of the fact that our country is not at present directly threatened, it can only be useful for these ideas on military problems to be set into motion at a time when they do not present a particular urgency. We have plenty of time to effect the indispensable reforms and these must necessarily be preceded by a phase of elaboration.

Therefore, the present study aims to open and outline this phase of elaboration and to assist those who have the heavy burden of providing France and Europe with military institutions which might, once again, constitute their safeguard in a time of danger.

Chapter I

AN INVENTORY OF THE PROBLEMS OF MODERN WARFARE

I. THE NUCLEAR MUTATION

It is trite to say that "warfare has changed". It has always been changing throughout history, but the development that is quite new and not well perceived by our contemporaries is that something quite beyond evolution has come about. We are witnessing a *mutation,* a mutation that provokes some people to say that "there will be no more war," a hope so often betrayed. It causes others to say that these changes do not in any way alter the basic nature of war. Both these views are true and false at the same time: there will probably not be other wars similar to those of the past (indeed, where now does one see sailboat navies and charging cavalry?) but there will also be new types of wars. On the other hand, as far as we can determine now, these new types of conflict will be so different from the old type that their basic form will follow principles quite alien to those which have governed warfare for several centuries. It is this revolution which must be understood.

The central element of this revolution is the appearance of nuclear weapons and, in general, of the potent means of destruction produced by scientific progress. Warfare conducted in accordance with both old concepts and modern weapons becomes a major catastrophe. Devised in this manner, it can no longer fulfill its historic role of an ordeal from God serving to resolve differences which resist diplomatic resolution. It would be an actual suicide and no longer the political tool termed by Clausewitz "the conduct of politics by other means". Then would mankind risk losing one of its most powerful restraints (the other being the iron rule of supply and demand) and the world frozen on political solutions which could not survive constant evolution. A new form of arbitration should be established.

Of course, mankind has dreamed for centuries of a world in which conflicts between nations would be resolved by arbitration through recourse to law. To this end, many noble minds have contributed solutions which were quickly found too unrealistic. There is no arbitration without established world law (we remain far from this goal) and, above all, without the existence of effective law enforcement. The present condition of the international community precludes recourse to such solutions except in cases of minor conflicts.

The renaissance of limited war

Under the circumstances described above and spontaneously, without developing new strategies, we have continued to resort to war (Korea, Indochina, Algeria, Vietnam, the Middle East, etc.) while instinctively seeking to achieve the political objective without courting the major risks feared by all. War is not extinct. It has changed its form and has become a type of confrontation in which the use of force is constantly held to be an acceptable—let us say bearable level—while, at the same time, exerting sufficient pressure to exact a political settlement. By trial and error, we are learning on a present-day scale a lesson known to our stone age ancestors. This knowledge is that human communities cannot co-exist without a few rules of the game. These rules create the opposite of the escalation principle observed by Clausewitz during the Napoleonic Wars and termed by him *"l'ascension aux extrêmes"* (rise to the extremes). In fact, the rules of the game reflect the unwillingness of a paroxysmic effort because of the absolute necessity of accepting only limited use of violence, which we can call limited warfare.

Characteristics of limited warfare in the nuclear age: "total strategy"

Limited warfare has been the predominant form of war throughout history and total wars have been rare. However, this same type of warfare is conducted today in an entirely new context due on one hand to nuclear deterrence, a phenomenon unknown until the present era and which we will need to carefully analyze. The other element of this context lies in the critical influence of modern mass communications and its almost decisive impact in the areas of national and international public opinion. Because of this peculiar context, modern limited warfare has an entirely new character.

The external characteristics are different today because of the generally held view that war presents a major risk. This imposes a restraint on the casual and fatalistic manner in which decisions to go to war were made in the past. The decision to have recourse to war, even a limited one, is no longer justified except in cases of extremely grave political tensions and only when one can expect to achieve the desired political objective without unacceptable catastrophe. Such a decision is arrived at with much more reflection than in earlier times and with very little of what Marxists call "military adventurism."

However, the greatest changes in warfare are found in their internal characteristics. In the old type of warfare, the aim in most cases was to exact a political settlement after a military victory. Military action was supposed to result in a psychological situation which would break the spirit of the enemy. When these strategies were no longer effective in obtaining such results, due generally to operational factors, the military effort was intensified—what we call escalation today—because its aim was a military victory through either increased military effort or decision for a war of attrition against the enemy. This is the phenomenon that Clausewitz called a "rise to the extremes". We have seen this pattern develop senselessly during the last two world wars. As I have already stated, it is this escalation spiral that has been effectively curtailed today to a level determined by moral and nuclear deterrence. Because of this deterrence, military war is no longer decisive in the proper sense of the word. The political decision, always a necessity, can only be brought about by a proper combination of limited military action and appropriate psychological, economic, and diplomatic activity. War strategy, which was governed in the past by military strategy and gave preeminence to military leaders, depends today upon a *total strategy* directed by heads of government and where military strategy plays only a subordinate role.

II. CONSTRAINTS OF TOTAL STRATEGY

That total strategy of limited war is now submitted to the constraints, sometimes complementary and sometimes opposed, of the modern means of communication and of the existence of nuclear weapons. There exist two important domains which need to be analyzed with great care and objectivity: mass media and domestic public opinion.

Modern news media have developed in such a way that events are instantaneously broadcast and commented upon, reaching an increasingly well-informed audience which is becoming conditioned to the style peculiar to the news media. These days, no event—especially a war—can be developed without having a wide consensus. The repeated experiences of two world wars followed by long and useless colonial wars have considerably helped to strip war of its glamour. This has come to the point in which youth in the West are convinced that war is not possible and that it is only a barbarism surviving from past centuries. Moreover, movies and especially television bring the reality of war from Vietnam direct into the living room to traumatize American homes. The same effects would have been the result had the Battle of Verdun been telecast into French homes during World War I. In presenting the horrors of war, modern news programs are inevitably pacifist and defeatist *per se.* This is a new phenomenon which is unlike the flag-waving and frequently childish posture the Press has taken in earlier wars.

However, today's news media reveal a completely different posture when they want to provoke indignation and enthusiasm for a cause by exploiting latent sentiments. In Western Europe, nationalist feelings that were predominant for the first half of the century have been abandoned today to a great extent. On the other hand, nationalist sentiment is quite strong in the Third World and even in the Communist bloc. Ideological, indeed racist and religious sentiment (Maoism, Guevaraism, anarchism, black power, arabism, islamism) holds full sway in the greater part of the globe. In general, we can believe that the present-day public is quicker to respond to ideological conflicts than to conflicts among nations. However, let us not forget that the German occupation of not quite thirty years ago elicited a resistance (admittedly a gradual one) that had its roots in the people of the nation. Wars between nations seem improbable at present, but a renewed outbreak would elicit a similar, no doubt delayed, reaction without fail. On the whole, let us say that the modern news media may in certain cases exert a truly hawkish influence (as now in Egypt and Israel) to prevent governments from accepting reasonable compromises, while at the same time, by presenting raw visions of war, they stir up sentiments which undermine the spirit of the communities involved in the hostilities.

This domestic involvement of the mass media is crucial because it molds public opinion to the point where war is acceptable to the public and it also demoralizes the public and makes compromise possible. Compromises are the only type of result possible in limited war. This is an element essential to the development of total strategy. It is an extremely delicate question because it of course depends rigidly on the mentality of the public and the degree of enforcement of laws governing the press. Bad propaganda may be damaging, while good propaganda may be decisive. We should not fear words: supposedly objective news always carries a more or less substantial amount of something we can call pure propaganda. The best propaganda is that which plays to public opinion and is the least detectable. Very capable newsmen can produce this propaganda if they are not blinded by preconceived political notions. Unfortunately, they are all too often blinded.

The mass media and world opinion: the "external maneuvers"

The influence of the mass media, crucial on the domestic scene, may also play a major role in regard to international public opinion. The truth is that nowadays any news item is immediately broadcast throughout the entire world. The result is that the various national opinions become interdependent in some respects: the various attitudes that exist in most countries react themselves either by hostile and even indignant feelings or by sympathy. It is through the nature of this instantaneous presence that news affects local political situations in foreign countries. Political or military involvements, revolutions or repressions all stir up sympathetic or hostile forces. These forces can play a considerable role in the conflict by applying moral suasion and by prodding governments to intervene. It was in this matter that very isolated local wars such as Biafra, Algeria and Vietnam had sizeable moral repercussions around the world, to the extent that reaction had seriously affected military action. In addition, the existence of various international organizations, of which the UN must rank as foremost, brings to bear very strong restraints on the antagonists. These include the more or less ad hoc organizations made up of mass movements such as the Congress for Peace and Vietnam peace groups. The result is a kind of psychological deterrence that we may call *moral deterrence* which would, for instance, prevent the antagonists from using certain types of weapons and from applying certain kinds of political control to the populations. The price of failing to observe these deterrents will be a hostile world opinion as in the case of the United States and its massive bombing of Vietnam. This same opinion will, in turn, bring about new practical restrictions such as limited bombing of supposedly military targets.

The effect of world opinion, which is so important today, is not really crucial unless it is able to undermine the antagonists' will to fight. The superpowers are aware of it, but may try to avoid its effect to a certain degree. We have seen a modest power such as Portugal withstand nearly universal hostility because its domestic opinion would not allow itself to be weakened, thanks to effective local controls. On the other hand, the Vietnamese experience has shown the combined restraining effect of a hostile world opinion and of a domestic press left free to practice traditions that systematically exploit sensationalism. This psychological aspect of war has become an essential factor of total strategy.

World opinion can do even more, at least under specially favorable circumstances. The Suez operation of 1956 was halted in great measure by a nearly unanimous vote of the United Nations General Assembly. This vote was passed because the two opposing mentors of the UN—the United States and the USSR—had for once aligned themselves and brought their combined pressure to bear on their dependents. Great Britain was experiencing intolerable pressures on the British pound at that time. France and Great Britain yielded. A similar vote after the Six-Day War had no effect on the Israelis because they were enjoying the backing of the United States at that moment. As we see by these examples, international pressures have an influential but not crucial role so long as world opinion remains fragmented and especially so long as the superpowers do not act in agreement with one another. All of this goes to show that we are still far from an equitable and effective arbitration mechanism.

All of these considerations stress the problems of managing news relating to instances of diplomatic activity. During the Algerian War, France failed completely in its moves in this sphere, because she followed the pretext that the question was an internal problem. In effect, and as I have stressed in *La Stratégie de l'Action,* the total strategy of modern war involves an *external effort* on the global scene. The scope of this activity may exceed that of purely military operations and may impose tight restrictions on the latter. The absolute necessity of such restrictions must be recognized.

Analysis of nuclear deterrence

The multifaceted and often ambiguous influence of the mass media is in part derived from the threat of nuclear war. This threat reinforces considerably the psychological impact of the media. Several years ago I completely analyzed the phenomenon of nuclear deterrence in *Dissuasion et Stratégie,* but I believe that it will be useful to discuss again a certain number of definitions that have become clear only in the last few years.

In order to lay a solid logical foundation, let us say first of all that nuclear deterrence is based on two essential but independent factors:

Existence of an adequate and effective *destruction capacity;*

Credibility regarding the potential use of this capacity.

In point of fact the deterrence of nuclear weapons lies in the threat that they may be *used.* The degree of effectiveness of the deterrence lies in the evaluation of this threat.

Evaluation of destructive capacity

The formation of an adequate and probably effective strike force brings up first of all a purely technical problem. It is necessary to build weapons and range vectors in order to assure a number of megatons, which would cause numerous deaths in population areas. In setting up their capacity, American theoreticians invented the "megadeath," a unit of measurement that represents one million potential deaths. Thus, strike capacity would be measured in terms of mega-deaths and it appears quite clear that even a fraction of one megadeath constitutes a suitable threat. The obvious cynicism of this logic has been considered scandalous by some people, as it certainly appears to be in its offensive aspects. This would be the case in the use of this threat against whole communities as a policy tool, as was the original intent. However, this point of view was abandoned nearly twenty years ago *because the nuclear threat became bilateral.*

From that time on this *unthinkable threat* became the only way to neutralize the opposing menace because we have not yet found the technical means to secure ourselves positively from nuclear destruction. The peoples of the opposing countries have become reciprocal *hostages* whose continued survival maintains the peace. It is the bilateral stance of the nuclear threat that gives nuclear weapons their deterrent effect. *It is the dialectic of opposing destruction capacities that gives rise to the phenomenon of deterrence.*

The implications of reciprocal threat: trends toward stability

Beginning with this conclusion we can draw out some logical implications that constitute a number of special problems.

The first and principal one is the *evaluation of destructive capacity.* At first we calculated according to existing weapons and delivery ranges. We determined their probable effectiveness with every technical correction allowing for margins of error, malfunction and enemy interception. We arrived in this manner at a destruction probability. This approach soon proved itself false, when we realized that striking first would not serve any purpose if the enemy were able to respond with devastating retaliation. We were discovering the substance of deterrence. A second phase of strategy planning focused on the possibility of possessing such a destruction capacity that a first strike would annihilate any enemy response capacity. This is what we have called *preemptive counterforce capacity.* But in this approach we quickly discovered considerable technological obstacles due to the survival tactics practiced by the nuclear powers. Around 1964 when these tactics had reached a high degree of effectiveness it became evident that the single deterrent value of a nuclear system depended on its retaliatory capacity after receiving a first strike from the enemy. The target of a second strike capacity can only be opposing population areas. Thus we have a counter-city capacity (or counter value). This is the situation at present.

It is in this state of affairs that we find another problem that is equally important. What was the balance between destruction capacities that would constitute deterrence in the dialectic of counter-city retaliatory capacity? Was either parity or superiority required? Perhaps a certain imbalance would still be a deterrent, and if so, to what degree? In all of this we came up against an essentially subjective problem which cannot be solved except in terms of a comparison between the risks and the stakes. What kind of political objective would allow acceptance of losses as high as several million deaths in a matter of hours? The evidence indicated that only extreme and nearly unimaginable situations would allow taking such a political decision. From that point it became clear that nuclear deterrence was extremely stable when the destruction capacity of the weaker power reached a low level of megadeaths, indeed even a single megadeath. Such a level is attainable with a relatively small number of thermonuclear weapons. Neither superiority nor parity were necessary any longer. Deterrence resulted from what Nixon calls "sufficiency". We could thus envision a halt to the arms race. Nuclear strategy was entering a diplomatic phase which resulted in the SALT talks. In the natural order of reasoning these talks should arrive at an accord.

Implications for stability inherent in the new nuclear strategy

In this development, however, we encountered ramifications that are extremely grave in their scope: at the moment when it became evident that nuclear deterrence was very stable, then reciprocal neutralization led to a general weapons imparity. As soon as the weaker power achieved sufficiency it became clear that nuclear deterrence neutralized only the nuclear level and that it had practically no effect on other levels. Nuclear war was beyond the realm of possibility, but *warfare in its other forms, notably in its diverse conventional forms, was no longer within the sphere of nuclear deterrence.* Moreover, even in the nuclear sphere deterrence could not really exist except between opposing nuclear systems. As General Gallois long ago had predicted, before it had come to be true, the guarantees of nuclear protection given by the nuclear parties to third, non-nuclear powers lost their practical value: the benefit of nuclear deterrence was reserved only for the nuclear powers that possess "sufficiency". Even for these same powers deterrence brought protection from nuclear attack but not from all other forms of attack. Thus after 25 years of effort and astronomical expenditures, we arrived at the semi-failure of nuclear strategy: all of this turned out as if the hopes we had placed in the new weapons had become vain ones. We would escape the "atomic death" whose prospect had stirred the sensitive minds of those scientists who were not sufficiently well informed on the realities of strategy. We lost, however, the ultimate weapon: that powerful antibiotic that, as we had once hoped, would impose an era of peace.

The attempt at psychological stabilization:
the retention of the escalation myth

Naturally the conclusion that I have developed here in its most basic and rudimentary form has been immediately obfuscated by a series of considerations more or less precise and convincing that had been already used in earlier phases, when reciprocal neutralization on the strategic nuclear level was beginning to appear possible. It was a case of proving that this material argument was not considering psychological factors and that nuclear deterrence remained intact since the recourse to nuclear weapons remained *credible* because of the ever present risk of *nuclear escalation.*

The risk of nuclear escalation was already an old story. In 1962 Herman Kahn dedicated his famous book, "On Escalation", to it. It was a nuclear version of Clausewitz's "tendency toward all-out war" in a rigorously controlled way. Recognizing the importance of the stakes, nuclear war would escalate progressively until it reached a decisive result. This theory—which at the conventional level dominated American Vietnam strategy, where it failed—was false in that it ignored the new imperatives of limited conflicts. The idea of automatic escalation has not proved itself anywhere. In the Middle East we have witnessed a reverse phenomenon. Indeed the possibility of escalation resulting from an accident or an irrational decision has continued to haunt the public mind, while strategists of different schools have endeavored to maintain an adequate degree of incertitude regarding the risk of escalation so that this residual doubt would maintain the deterrent effect on the other levels.

The first of these are the Soviets, who at an early stage took a radical position: nothing would dissuade them from using their nuclear weapons when attacked. Their fundamental doctrine, which was disseminated in Sokolowski's book, "Military Strategy", conceived war as a violent nuclear exchange from which the USSR must emerge victorious regardless of its losses. It is difficult to determine if this position represents a sincere conviction (which would be naive) or if it involves a psychological effort directed to the Soviet military and public and to potential enemies as well. In any case, a doctrine as radical as this nourishes the doubt that continues deterrence. General de Gaulle repeatedly took a similar position.

The Americans under McNamara tried to maintain the credibility of their deterrence strategy with the complicated flexible response doctrine which in effect again declared the possibility of limited atomic war, because the threat of annihilation would constrain the enemy to reject nuclear escalation. In McNamara's own and rather ambiguous terms, this could be "damage limitation through insured destruction capacity". As ingenious as this thesis was, it was not very coherent: damage limitation stemmed in part from potential counter-force action that assumed a first strike capacity, in fact unattainable. Insured destruction threat is no more credible than the credibility of retaliation, which means practically zero in a state of reciprocal insured destruction capacity. In reality and in spite of Sokolowski's bluster, flexible response tended to convince the Soviets that a potential war could remain limited and confine itself to a theatre

outside American and Soviet territories. As far as possible it would develop
according to conventional warfare methods. However, the fear that a misunder-
standing could cause the Soviets to unleash the massiveness of Sokolowski's
strategy led the Americans to rule out in practice the use of tactical nuclear
weapons except in the event of a very grave situation. To justify this strategy
Kennedy issued a pressing and futile appeal to the Europeans to increase their
conventional forces. At the same time American representatives provided docu-
mentation to show that the superiority of NATO conventional strength would
allow confrontation with Soviet conventional forces.

III. IMPLICATIONS FOR NATO

Naturally this thesis met with a cool reception in Europe where the great
hope for security lay with the strategic nuclear umbrella. Instinctively Europeans
preferred a peace maintained by the threat of a global catastrophe to the
prospect of a limited war in Europe. After confusing debates that were muddled
even more by France's departure from NATO, it was decided that the official
NATO strategy was that of flexible response. Hardly anyone in Western Europe
understood the true nature of flexible response. Because of its complexity and
obscurity, it satisfied everybody. The Germans desperately attached themselves
to the "forward strategy" and to the American strategic nuclear umbrella. It
satisfied the British and Mr. Helmut Schmidt who feared above all else the
premature use of nuclear weapons. It also satisfied the Belgians and the Dutch
who were pleased to feel protected by an international system, which involved
partnership with the Americans.

Unfortunately for those in America and notably in France who had been able
to reach a more objective analysis, it appeared that NATO's whole strategic
concept (a contradictory combination of a succession of strategies) did not
represent an effective concept. Happily the Soviet-American detente made this
less disturbing. The "forward strategy" dear to the Germans had become in fact
a true potential suicide since the use of tactical nuclear weapons at the onset of
possible hostilities was no longer anticipated. Air forces deployed far forward to
deliver atomic weapons at the onset in a preemptive capacity were temporarily
exposed. The American nuclear guarantee which was supposed to insure the
security of the group, melted as snow in the sun as the SALT talks constructed
an increasing and practically absolute stability on the strategic level. In addition,
developments in American politics constrained the Nixon Administration to
reduce its forces in Europe. It became evident that a reappraisal of strategy was
becoming imperative. This is the situation that we are in.

IV. CONCLUSIONS

After this long analysis we can present a few solid conclusions and propose an
outline for studies:

1. Nuclear deterrence and the mass media have completely dominated recent developments in warfare. The impact of these new factors is still subject to conflicting interpretations, which accounts for the uncertainties. In spite of this, it seems quite clear that the only indisputable role of strategic nuclear deterrence is that of neutralizing the hostile nuclear threat. Extended deterrence for third powers has still only an undefined value. The problem of sustaining and extending the scope of strategic deterrence is the first aim of this book.

2. However we are very far from a return to the conventional warfare of the pre-atomic period. The fringe of fear around nuclear escalation (which has been encouraged by the mass media with all its psychological tools) and the independent development of moral deterrence creates a new atmosphere for conventional warfare. While theoretically possible (that is to say, it is not strictly ruled out by nuclear deterrence), conventional warfare is checked by a series of different restraints. The natural modern form of conventional war is the *limited war*. The strength of the checks that apply to conventional war may be considerable in certain cases—for example, the war in the Middle East. This gives entirely new characteristics to conventional war as seen by developments in the Cold War and by the frequent recourse to guerrilla war methods. Conventional war must be reexamined in order to adapt it to these new conditions. This will be the second aim of this book.

3. The situation remains in which conventional war, which was impossible ten years ago except in those geographic areas (principally in Europe) where the nuclear powers had important interests, is no longer really barred by nuclear deterrence. This means there is a *gap* in the deterrence system that must be filled because if political circumstances bring on a conflict in Europe, it would be an extremely dangerous situation regardless of intentions to limit that conflict. We must therefore reestablish the conventional war deterrent in the most dangerous areas. In the state of our recent technical capacity this refers to the *threat* of early tactical nuclear weapons. The ways and means of a potential use of tactical weapons and the restoration of the credibility of such a use will constitute the third aim of this book.

4. Finally, acknowledging current trends in military technology, it is evident that the data given on deterrence and the evolution of warfare toward limited forms will bring important implications to our view of the armed forces. This difficult subject will be the fourth aim of the book.

Chapter II

THE LEVEL OF
STRATEGIC NUCLEAR DISSUASION

After the various considerations brought forward in the preceding chapter concerning strategic nuclear deterrence, it might seem that the topic has been completely discussed. However, it has only been considered from the point of view of its external and global aspects. In order to understand the nature and the scope of this phenomenon, it is necessary to recognize its internal factors and their influence. Then one may discover the tendencies that direct its evolution as well as the limitations imposed in this field, today upon the medium powers, tomorrow upon the superpowers.

I. UNCERTAINTY AND PRIORITY OF TECHNIQUE

Strategic nuclear deterrence is an implicit phenomenon the effect of which depends on the subjective estimation of technical results which have not been tested in their real setting. This explains its highly speculative character. All such speculations are based upon scientific observation of technical improvements made by the enemy and one's own technical improvements. One subsequently endeavors to imagine what the consequences of these improvements would be if a real conflict should arise. A large degree of accuracy at the beginning leads, at the end, to a large degree of uncertainty.

Thus, when strategic deterrence was originally based on the airplane, the basic technical problems consisted in the accuracy of firing, penetration capacity and interception capacity of aircraft. The result is a technical war involving aircraft, radar and navigation aid equipment. Without dropping a single bomb, billions have been spent in an effort to increase the speed and maximum flying altitude of fighter bombers, to increase the maximum range of radar, and to develop anti-aircraft firing possibilities. Planes played hide-and-seek with radar, ground-skimming navigation methods were improved and aircraft were equipped with long range interception devices, as well as with long range nuclear devices, enabling them to penetrate into enemy zones where aircraft interception had become a too-dangerous probability. A whole range of technical electronical devices for jamming enemy guidance radar systems was developed. Penetration and deception tactics were perfected. In times of peace, the improvements of one side dated the other's equipment at a cost of billions of dollars. Technical escalation, the nuclear form of Clausewitz's "ascent to the extremes", was the tunic of Nessus in thriving economies. Each of these improvements seemed to be decisive, but only for a short period of time. Only exceptionally and by chance could partial experimentations be enacted. Thus, the penetration capacity of American aircraft could be tested by the U2 secret missions over the USSR, until it was shot down. By the same token, the efficiency of American electronic counter measures and penetration tactics was tested in the Tonkin area in the face of the Soviet SAM 2 interception system. However, on the whole, possible results of a nuclear confrontation remained very uncertain. As a matter of fact, this uncertainty worked to the advantage of deterrence, as it could not ensure the inefficacy of the means of attack. . .

With the development of intercontinental rockets and space techniques, the technological race took on new, dizzying dimensions. The ICBM made completely obsolescent the entire system of antiaircraft defense which had been realized at great cost by the United States and NATO. The problem concerning interception, which had to be resolved within a very short period of time, required new materials and the use of electronic computers. The old duel between penetration and interception was restaged again, but on a larger scale. Penetration endeavored to deceive interception by using various devices, such as variable trajectory vehicles or even satellized orbital vehicles. From there, the Multiple Independent Reentry Vehicles (MIRV) were derived, capable of reaching several independent targets, thus increasing the number of offensive weapons while complicating the task of defense. Defense, which already had a potential interception capacity that was of unknown value but that was not non-existent, scored a point with the use of high precision guidance procedures developed during the conquest of the Moon. It is estimated that, under these conditions, the Probable Error Circle (PEC) can be reduced to approximately 200 meters, which puts the concrete silos of the Minuteman vehicles at the mercy of a single blow. Under these conditions, defense recovered an important capacity against forces in the case of a pre-emptive attack. The United States countered with the installation of an anti-missile system which protected the silos. At the same time, the problem of locating targets for destruction, allotted to the U2 aircrafts during the aircraft period, was entrusted to observation satellites. These took infrared pictures of the enemy zone and transmitted their photographs by television,[1] just as it was done for the lunar tests. A permanent observation of extensive areas of the USSR and the United States would obviously have required a number of satellites impossible to be maintained in times of peace. Furthermore, as inter-continental transmissions—and, consequently, the alert—required numerous communication satellites, the interception and destruction of satellites became an urgent strategic problem. The escalation of technique after the aircraft phase developed into a phase of space war. *All this to maintain a conjectural deterrence!* The race became more and more absurd.

II. ATTEMPTED DIPLOMATIC LIMITATION AND CONFRONTATION OF OPPOSED STRATEGIES

This situation showed how necessary it was to reach an agreement with the Soviet Union and negotiation had become possible since the political atmosphere between the United States and the Soviet Union had appreciably cleared up. After a series of preliminary contacts (Pugwash, Treaty on the Prohibition of Nuclear Explosions in the Atmosphere, Treaty on Non-proliferation) the SALT negotiations could finally begin.

The primary interest of this negotiation was to allow the opposing parties to appraise their respective intentions and to better understand their strategies. Each read the other's works, but both had their own prejudices. The American strategy directed against cities was considered by the Soviet Union as a concept intended to veil the preparation of a surprise attack capable of breaking Soviet resistance by a shattering blow. A peace agreement based upon a menace of mutual destruction (which was the American theory) seemed unrealistic to them and, therefore, suspicious. Consequently, the Soviet strategy stressed mainly means of protection and defense, in order to ensure a large extent of combat capability to the Soviet Union after having received a severe first strike from the enemy. Sokolowski's "rodomontades" are to be explained by this

---

[1] There are other techniques, notably the periodic release of rolls of film.

essential concern. Furthermore, if such a surprise attack could be foreseen in time, Soviet forces would be ready to precede the enemy attack by a series of nuclear, airborne, land and sea operations. They could therefore field a large offensive capacity using a mobility sufficient to seize enemy territories, thus constituting a relative protection for their own forces. This Soviet strategy, however, was mainly characterized by the fact that it was directed "against forces" and not, as the United States proclaimed, "against cities." In the offensive (ICBM, MRBM, tactical atomic weapons) as well as in the defensive part (anti-aircraft defense, anti-missile missiles, passive protection, evacuation of cities), the main objective consisted in safeguarding a maximum combat capacity and the survival of Soviet forces and populations. Could such a strategy be efficient? It would be doubtful in the case of a "spasm war." On the other hand, it must be admitted that, in the case of a limited nuclear war, the concept could be very useful, even decisive, whereas nothing analogous existed on the American side.

Because of this, American concepts have gone through a period of uncertainty. Clearly, American supporters of an anti-missile defense system are gathering more strength. It would now appear indispensable to possess balanced strength in imitation of the Soviets, both offensive and defensive: in order to discuss "parity," it is necessary that there be equivalence, therefore that strategies be similar. The pact of mutual suicide on the basis of the American concept must make room for a parallel limitation of forces capable of carrying on a "non-spasmodic" nuclear war according to the Soviet concept. It is a great innovation from the American point of view in relation to the principles which had triumphed during the Kennedy era. Moreover we can ask ourselves whether the Soviet concepts are quite realistic or if they do not constitute a resurgence of the American strategic ideas of the 1950s. Also, certain American theoreticians go so far as to envisage a pact of a new character: the commitment not to be the first to use nuclear arms ("no first use"), a principle already proclaimed by the Chinese. The value of such a pact could be to reassure the Soviets in regard to their suspicions of seeing the Americans prepare a surprise attack. But does it really reassure if political trust is not reestablished?

In a definitive sense, after the partial agreements of limitation on the deployment of anti-missiles and on the number of ICBMs and MIRVs, it is probable that the SALT negotiations will conclude more on the basis of declarations of intentions rather than on technical agreements which are in any case unverifiable—even if the Soviets were to end by admitting a system of reciprocal control, which is completely improbable. The SALT negotiations, if they succeed, will come upon an essentially political accord only if the factors which are external to the negotiations permit it. It will be a *de facto* armistice between the two super-greats which will prove that their policies are no longer incompatible. This is the most probable and most favorable prospect. It would have important consequences.

III. STRATEGIC CONSEQUENCES

The first consequence, already mentioned in the previous chapter, but this time irrefutable, would be to remove all credibility from the guarantee offered to allies by the American atomic umbrella ("extended deterrence"). It should be especially noted that the protection offered by anti-missiles (ABMs), if they are developed, allows only for the reduction to a certain percentage (10 per cent, 20 per cent, to the top maximum of 50 per cent) of the losses to be expected in a nuclear war. Reciprocal deterrence therefore remains complete as does the paralysis of the nuclear level. The American strategic nuclear system covers the United States, the Soviet nuclear system covers the USSR. If political conditions impose or recommend covering another geographical zone (Europe, Japan, or India, for example), it becomes necessary to equip these zones of strategic nuclear forces with autonomous deterrence. The Soviet-American accord necessarily leads to a certain limited proliferation and, therefore, to the creation of new forces, a problem which I will later examine.

Another consequence, much more immediate, is to completely liberate the conventional level from all nuclear deterrence. This liberation, which is already implicit in the present strategic situation, would become explicit in case of an agreement on the principle of "no first use" of nuclear arms. We would actually be coming back to the situation which existed before the nuclear age and, therefore, to the organic instability of opposing military systems. This prospect is especially dangerous in Europe, at least as long as political instability continues there. Under these conditions, it becomes necessary to find a means of creating a new form of deterrence for conventional warfare.

The solution of this problem can be researched by three quite different methods.

The first consists of coming back to the traditional formula of the conventional armament race. Historical experience (1914, 1939) is not very encouraging and I believe that I demonstrated in *Dissuasion et Stratégie* that the conventional armament race would carry with it a growing instability, because of the hopes of victory it would develop. Therefore, the solution could not be very good. But it is not out of our reach: Western Europe with its 200 million inhabitants and more, a GNP greater than that of the USSR, has the material means to equip its important conventional forces, equal or even superior to those of the USSR. Naturally, such an effort would not be possible unless Europe felt really threatened. As in the USSR, it would only cut the standard of living. Moreover, this enormous effort, if it were agreed to, would lead to extremely unstable strategic formulations, as we shall see in detail in the chapter on the level of conventional warfare, notably because of the high costs of conventional arms that we have today, narrowly limiting their volume. In conclusion, this traditional formula which Kennedy recommended is by far the least certain and the most costly. It is, on the contrary, the routine which confers a certain degree of probability. . . .

The second method, which I call "the Chinese formula", is that of the organization of peoples' militia to prepare for a general interior resistance. After all, Western Europe, in its entirety, is vast enough to permit a strategy of this kind, already established in certain countries like Yugoslavia. However, it presupposes a moral preparation of the population from which we are quite distant. It is not very probable that the opinion of developed countries would be ready to consent to the sacrifices and enormous destruction which this kind of defense would necessarily bring with it from the start. Although credible for countries which are, like China, still primitive and revolutionary, this method would have little for our countries. This does not mean that a prolonged occupation would not, in the long run, raise a very serious armed resistance, such as occurred against the Germans. The Chinese formula has a real deterrent value for China. Its operational effectiveness was shown in Vietnam. It would seem inapplicable as such in Western Europe. On the contrary, as we will see further on, in the chapter on militias, there are real possibilities in the militia concept which could be exploited by developed countries for the purpose of forming, at a minimum cost, a military system capable of complementing adequately the system of traditional conventional forces, necessarily very limited in volume. This will be one of the interesting conclusions of the present study.

The third method is that which the Americans had previewed in the 1950s: it is the *threat of the use* of tactical atomic weapons. This method, explicitly provided by Soviet doctrine and effectively prepared within the framework of NATO, met with great disfavor in the United States during the 1960s because of the risks of nuclear escalation attributed to it. It should be recognized today that these risks have become minimal due to the great stability of the strategic nuclear level. From another point of view, while the Soviets envisage conducting actual battle with tactical atomic arms, we will later see that this idea meets considerable difficulties and that the surest result of more or less generalized use of tactical atomic arms on the battlefield would be to create completely unpredictable situations. In fact, no aggressor would be able to pride himself on conducting such a battle, which no one has ever experienced and in which the nerves of troops, as well as commanders, would be sorely tested. In these conditions, *the threat* of the use of atomic weapons on the battlefield would not fail to have an almost *completely deterrent effect,* as much because of the uncertainty of the results as the residual risks of escalation—improbable as they are. It would thus be the surest and currently most accessible means of reestablishing a serious deterrent against conventional warfare. This idea is not new, as we know, but it has been in large part obscured by the arguments made with regard to the flexible response when strategic deterrence had a sufficient value. It meets violent opposition as much in the United States (from adherents of "no first use") as in Germany and Great Britain where the fear of atomic destruction maintains a sort of mystique from what has been called the raising of the nuclear threshold. In this discussion, which we will take up in more detail, few people see that it is not a question of use, but of the threat of use; that it is not a question of combat, but of deterrence; just as it is moreover at the strategic nuclear level, which, however, does not raise any opposition. If common sense still possesses some convincing value, it is this solution which could prevail, at least as long as European political problems keep their present instability.

As we have just seen, the neutralization of the strategic nuclear level raises some important and difficult problems. It is necessary to return the deterrent value to the conventional level which it is about to lose. A completely new strategy, bringing with it a new concept of forces, has now become inevitable.

IV. THE PROBLEM OF THE NUCLEAR BUILDUP OF AUTONOMOUS STRATEGIC FORCES AND TECHNICAL LEVELS

The buildup of autonomous nuclear forces does not seem to pose any major problems in our day. France and China, by groping a little, have shown us the way to be followed. China, like the USSR, has benefited from more or less clandestine information on nuclear techniques. France, through fully autonomous research, has resolved alone the essential problems of the nuclear arms industry. Japan, Israel, Germany, and even India could potentially do the same. We know in a rough sense what this would cost and that it would not be exorbitant, in spite of what everyone says. It is a decision that is within reach of middle powers. Naturally, it is not logical unless it is a question of dissuading an eventual adversary. Moreover, it is a decision of considerable political value, fully in contradiction to the Treaty of Non-Proliferation, but, to my mind, it corresponds quite well to the present phase of evolution of the nuclear situation, when political tensions serious enough to justify it exist.

Once this decision has been reached, one has to resolve a host of difficult problems. France, in her limited efforts, has had to evolve and create three generations of arms systems: first the airplane, then the surface-to-surface rocket of medium range, then the sea-to-surface rocket-carrying nuclear submarine. The explosives were, at first, nuclear, but are in the process of becoming thermonuclear. In the present stage of evolution and as temporarily as always in technical matters, it seems good that the nuclear submarine, because of its survival capacity, is the most dissuasive weapon. However, the appearance of anti-missiles poses technical problems of penetration which could require new efforts, perhaps very costly ones. Finally, the aerial defense of France could not be resolved except in the larger—and more technical—framework of NATO.

This experience shows that the building of an autonomous nuclear force, relatively easy in the beginning, very quickly encounters a technical and financial wall which can only be surmounted by first-ranking powers like the United States and the USSR. At that point, strategic deterrence appears to present two distinct technical levels: "level 1" corresponding to an advanced science and technology but having only limited financial means at its disposal, and "level 0" corresponding to the military application of a very elaborate science, technically and financially capable of exploring and utilizing the most advanced areas of research.

In the present state of technology, in order to reach "level 0" a nation has to be able to have ready:

1. a deterrent system of intercontinental weapons (ICBM), multiple warhead weapons (MIRV) and anti-missile missiles (ABM);

2. a network of reconnaissance satellites (inhabited satellites included);

3. a network of communication satellites;

4. a system for interception of hostile satellites.

The building of such networks implies that one has reached the point of resolving the problems raised by the production of thrust, the miniaturization of material and the precision of advanced electronics. The cost of a network of reconnaissance satellites is very high, since to attain its full advantage, this system demands a high frequency of launchings. The inhabited satellites, whose realization is more onerous, would be of much higher effectiveness. Inhabited or not, satellites require the existence of launching or guidance bases quite widely located throughout the world.

As we saw above, this "level 0", because of its galloping technology, tends to surpass the possibilities of the superpowers, hence the SALT negotiations. However, the present state of technical capability allows the superpowers a sure superiority over those possessing "level 1".

Is this to say that "level 1" is ineffective? This is the big argument of the adversaries (political) of the French nuclear force. Now, it must be said with conviction, that "level 1", even incomplete, remains extremely formidable. Of course because of the "level 0", the penetrations are uncertain but this incertitude itself is dissuasive, because a very limited number of thermonuclear weapons crossing the defenses of the adversary would represent a considerable threat. Only vital political stakes would permit the acceptance of such risks. Moreover, it should be emphasized that the nuclear constellation carries with it a certain interdependence of the different parts which it forms. Nuclear deterrence starting from the moment that there are more than two players, is never really bilateral. The reciprocal action of this multilateral situation tends to establish a situational solidarity between nuclear nations; an attack on Japan by the USSR would have a hard time leaving the United States and China unaffected, just as an attack on Europe would. Nuclear aggression revealing a political design of the greatest cynicism would constitute an alarm signal of the greatest seriousness which *could* justify some pre-emptive action on the part of the other great power. This possibility, even uncertain, confers a notable deterrent capacity to the forces of "level 1" and a sure guarantee of survival.

Finally, and it is here we open a veritable Pandora's box, the existence of nuclear weapons can lead to forms of conflict which are very different from those which the Americans have provided and brought up to date. Nuclear guerrilla warfare, conducted with artisans' weapons, would be an extremely dangerous form of international terrorism. It is, moreover, this prospect (we shall return to it) that will sooner or later force solutions prohibiting nuclear proliferation in a practical sense.

All in all, it can be concluded that "level 1", in spite of its deficiencies with regard to "level 0", allows for the attainment of a very serious degree of deterrence as soon as it attains a certain minimum volume, a degree of deterrence which is more effective in another way than indirect deterrence (extended deterrence), which the strategic nuclear deterrence of the superpowers claims to achieve. This is the reason why there are great chances that it will be developed in the coming years, at least on a limited scale. An evident disadvantage of "level 1" is that, although it is founded on the simplest possible technical formulas, it is to be feared that it might evolve quite rapidly towards the techniques of "level 0", while the latter will continue their escalation toward the most advanced techniques. I think that at this stage, it is a temptation which one should know how to put aside: one nation which equips itself with a relatively primitive means of deterrence technically speaking and, thanks to the doubt which remains about its effectiveness, assures itself a certain degree of security. We should know how to content ourselves with this "certain degree", which to my mind corresponds to the aimed-at political goal. At this point, the created deterrence, purely "counter-city", does not allow for waging a limited nuclear war like the systems of "level 0", in which the offensive and defensive equipment is combined. It is a means of war. It is, above all, a political weapon in the regions of the world wherein tensions need to be stabilized and it is much better this way, since it limits possible adventurism.

As for the practical formation of a nuclear force at "level 1", it can be effected according to very different formulas. According to the method used by France and China, we can imagine that all of the techniques are rediscovered through national means. It is the most independent and also the most expensive formula. Another method would consist of buying all or part of the equipment and techniques from the States which possess them.

The formula is much less expensive, but notably less independent. Finally, the existence of the formula initiated in Europe in 1957 cannot be neglected; in it, the Americans stockpiled nuclear arms under their control, ready to be delivered to their allies in case of aggression. This formula, by far the least expensive, has the disadvantage of placing the decision of use, and therefore of deterrence, in the hands of the power (or international organization) who is the holder of nuclear weapons. Its credibility may be weak, but its deterrent impact is not nil.

Other formulas have been imagined, such as, for example, diffusing only defensive nuclear arms (ABM). Taking into account that these arms could procure only a very partial protection, it can be said that its deterrent effect— and therefore its political stabilizing effect—would be very weak, if not nil.

V. PROSPECTS FOR EVOLUTION

We have seen that the present strategic juncture was leading to a revision of concepts, to the probable building of autonomous strategic nuclear forces of a local character. At the same time, a larger and larger doubt was becoming apparent surrounding the established good of technical escalation which seemed to be the fatal consequence of the principle of nuclear deterrence. From these contradictory tendencies, what can we deduce about the general evolution of this major problem?

There is no subject that has exercised more attention on the imagination of researchers since the Baruch report of 1945 or 1946 calling for the international-ization of nuclear arms. Today we find ourselves confronted with a variety of solutions: the nuclear monopoly of the United States and the USSR, a formula surpassed in actuality; contractual or authoritarian limitation of nuclear powers by the formula of the Treaty of Non-proliferation probably already null and void; the general suppression of nuclear arms and their prohibition, a formula which always constitutes the official objective of Soviet and French policy; the "no first use" of nuclear arms which is the official theory of the Chinese and the contractual limitation of offensive and defensive nuclear arms, a formula of the SALT negotiations. Naturally, one can think of a number of other formulas.

I, myself, in *Dissuasion et Stratégie* set forth another prospect, much more ambitious, but naturally inapplicable at the moment. This prospect is quite utopian and, at first glance, seems to be confirmed by the technical evolution which we have noticed. This relates in a way to the Marxist doctrine of historical materialism, the restraints growing out of technical progress. Today, a large number of technical problems cannot be resolved except in a global framework: space, the appropriation of sea depths, modern telecommunications, control of intercontinental weapons, monetary systems, etc., etc. . . . These constraints will necessarily create world institutions (probably in the framework of the United Nations, whose competence and authority will not cease to grow). In reality, the tendency of modern technology is toward globalization, a tendency which will perhaps predominate in the 21st century, but which we only now perceive. Thus, the historical period in which we live would only be an intermediate period between the age of Nation-States and a future age with some world unity exercising a more or less restraining authority over the Nation-States. It is possible that in the course of this evolution, which raises the serious problem of knowing what will be the civilization to inspire and organize this globalization, we will pass through a phase of "great unions" of confronted continents, each seeking to have its own solutions prevail. In any case, the outcome of this influence battle, which seems to me will be the essential happening of the 21st century, cannot fail to lead to a very serious political crisis. It would be interesting to see if the world were being organized on an American, Soviet, Chinese, Japanese or European model. Perhaps there will be a synthesis such as already announces itself in the religious domain. Perhaps, on the contrary, there will be inexpiable battles, a new "last conflict" before a possible final stage of explosion.

This somewhat apocalyptic vision of the future is usually challenged by the politologues who uphold the diversity of humanity, as well as by those who justly consider the Nation to be the natural cell—the basic structure of humanity—at a time when so many young nations are born into independence. But in this very theoretical debate, the error would be to see globalization replace the centralized nation which we know. World authority cannot be conceived of unless based on other structures strictly limited by indisputable technical necessity.

From this point of view, we can imagine that, several decades from now, the system of strategic nuclear deterrence could derive from a world authority, the nations certainly keeping their armed forces and even perhaps a purely defensive deterrence of the "level 1" type if it should still be necessary. Such a result could not come about without numerous ups and downs. These could be very serious, and above all, decisive. This is why the general problems set forth here, in spite of their speculative character, must not be misunderstood.

The present world creates new formulae. Let us be attentive in order to discern them, foresee their evolution, and arm ourselves ahead of time against the dangers they carry.

Chapter III

THE LEVEL
OF CONVENTIONAL WARFARE

From all the preceding considerations and particularly from those having to do with strategic nuclear deterrence, we find that conventional military warfare remains today a more or less probable possibility, even in areas where it has been considered prohibited by strategic nuclear deterrence. If on this last point, very happily, no experimental verification has been produced, we possess enough examples of conventional military war since the birth of the atomic age to affirm that classic military warfare can still occur.

However, as I have been emphasizing from the first chapter on, the phenomenon of conventional warfare has changed profoundly both in its means and its ends, certainly because of technical and psychological evolution, but also, and perhaps especially, because of the limited character which total contemporary strategy imposes on military warfare. It is therefore absolutely necessary to proceed to an internal analysis of conventional warfare in order to grasp its essential characteristics. This will be the purpose of the present chapter.

I. DEFINITION OF CONVENTIONAL WARFARE

It is perhaps not futile to define conventional warfare, for up to the present it has taken very different forms. There have been battles between organized armies such as those of World War II (Korea, the Six-Day War, the episode of Bizerte); there have been other wars which put in opposition classic forces of different types of guerillas (Indochina, Algeria, Vietnam, etc.). Badly defined forms of classic warfare have been observed which were characterized by an extreme limitation of ground combat, while in the aerial sphere a kind of battle went on which tended merely to demonstrate a certain technical superiority (the Israeli-Arab war on the Suez Canal in 1970). It is probable that other forms will appear (how should we, after all, classify the war in Biafra?).

In this situation, it appears that the only common characteristic of these different examples is that they are *wars carried on with conventional arms.* That is to say that they are carried on without nuclear arms. The limited use by the Americans of chemical weapons in Vietnam does not contradict this definition because it was a matter of classical chemical weapons already in use during the First World War, excluding chemical or bacteriological weapons capable of producing mass destruction and which, because of this capability, could have consequences which are analogous to those of nuclear arms.

Naturally, these conventional weapons, developed from those of World War II, have progressed considerably in all spheres. The innovations are numerous, notably: helicopters, ground-air weapons, portable surface-to-surface missiles, remote control anti-tank weapons, the enormous progress of aerial fire capacity; but also the increase of power in portable arms, the increased perfection of tanks and the means of crossing, etc. Each innovation carries with it important consequences: the permanent dispersion of formations, the probable decline of battle tanks which are heavily armed and armour-plated, the development of aero-mobile action, a change in the characteristics of what we call aviation. Two other technical characteristics of modern forces seem to bring with them important changes in the form of operations. First, the reduction of the volume of conventional forces because of the high price of modern weaponry, and the increased mobility of those forces, thanks to full motorization and aerial transport. These two characteristics lend to the maneuver accrued possibilities which one must know how to exploit.

But at the same time, we have seen the birth and the development of combat methods which lend a completely new effectiveness to guerilla warfare. In the Indochina War, in Vietnam and Algeria, as well as in China during the Second World War, the confrontation between mobile, primitive and lightly armed forces and the most powerfully armed classic forces, has shown that, in favorable terrain and in certain psychological conditions, guerilla warfare succeeded in defeating forces which were much more powerful. There is a perfectionization of the procedures of revolutionary war which I have examined in detail in *La Guerre Révolutionaire,* which will, at this point, certainly have an important impact on conventional warfare, at least every time the necessary conditions are present.

It is no doubt difficult to arrange a synthesis which takes into account the simultaneous action of different factors of which the relative amounts would constitute the different forms of conventional warfare. What will certainly be common to all of these forms will be:

on the one hand, the use of conventional weapons;

on the other hand, the more or less major limitation on the military effort and even on the use of power for reasons relating to total strategy.

However, it will be no doubt inevitable that we analyze, one by one, the most characteristic forms.

II. ANALYSIS OF TRADITIONAL CONVENTIONAL WARFARE

The conflict between more or less modernized armed conventional forces responds to a logic that should be well known, but that has been obscured by too many theories systematically founded on experiences which are too recent and too particular. I showed in *La Guerre Révolutionnaire* how primitive warfare had evolved towards siege warfare and pitched battle and, in *l'Introduction à la Stratégie,* I analyzed the successive formulae of interaction between operations and the battle, the decisive battle being the supreme goal, but often out of reach of the belligerents. All through history the art of war has consisted of forcing the adversary to take on a battle in conditions which were not favorable to him and then to *destroy* his forces in a decisive battle which actually consisted of further disorganizing the enemy forces by an action which caused the moral collapse of the enemy command and troops. According to these technical givens, we have successively witnessed operations which were almost powerless in forcing into battle, and then (beginning with Napoleon) operations in preparing and keeping in battle. In the nineteenth century, the increase of fire power led to giving a progressively larger combat capacity to operational formations, to such an extent that operations and battles were confused. In 1914–18 and in 1940 the saturation at the fronts had suppressed the operations preliminary to the battle. On the contrary, it was the initial battle, decisive with difficulty in 1914–18 and easily decisive in 1940, which permitted that it be taken full advantage of in later operations.

This analysis, which has the advantage of showing the final goal of the action to be reached by immediate means, is insufficient in that it does not take into account the initiative of the adversary. Because of this, and according to the particular situation, it will be necessary first of all to ward off the action of the adversary, wear away his forces and his morale, indeed, force the enemy to use up his reserves, before being able to undertake the decisive action. In other cases (Sinai 1967, France 1940) the enemy presents himself in formation which permits the battle to be opened with the decisive action.

The essence of conventional warfare will then be the *fencing* done by the two adversaries with a view to obtaining the disorganization of each other's forces. It is this fencing that we will analyze by considering, first of all, the factors of the fencing, then the characteristics which they impress upon the modern maneuver.

The factors of the fencing

Operational fencing is dominated by three main factors, which are themselves quite complex: the volume and the quality of the forces; the space of the operational theater; the estimated power of the classic firearms, both land and aerial.

The volume and quality of the forces

They bring to light, as always, the problem which presents quality and quantity. Today, in spite of the progress of national incomes and industrial production, it is necessary to narrowly limit the volume of quality arms because they have become too expensive. Even in serious political circumstances, it is not a question of equipping in modern fashion vast armies such as was done in the First World War and—indeed a little less—in the Second World War. *Modern forces (aerial, anti-aerial and mechanized) are necessarily very reduced in volume.* Let us say that they are without a doubt equal in volume to one-tenth of that which they were in 1940. If recourse to larger forces is desired, it is then necessary to accept the fact that the quality of the equipment will be considerably less. It is therefore necessary to sacrifice mobility and fire power. This use of second-class forces, normal in revolutionary warfare and quite common in the Second World War, has not until now been taken into consideration by Western armies. This represents a gap to which we will return in our discussion.

The space of the operational theater

This is generally such that it exceeds by far the tactical possibilities of existing forces as they have been conceived. In effect, it is necessary not only to furnish a "front", effectively covering the area facing the endangered direction, but also to hold on to all the area of the theater in order to assure control against aero-mobile actions and revolutionary warfare. The result of this disparity between the volume of forces and the space to be defended is to revive the situation of armies before the great development of national armies, thanks to mobilization and mechanical methods of logistic support. Either you spread the existing forces in width and in depth in order to protect the area, in which case they no longer possess any offensive or defensive power; or you concentrate them in one part of the theater, thus leaving open considerable areas; or, finally, you constitute a series of concentrated forces separated by open areas which the adversary can take advantage of. This situation, which was that of armies before 1914, was acceptable because the two adversaries benefited only from a limited mobility in relation to the space, the mobility of the infantry or the cavalry. The maneuver, which was slowed down by this fact, allowed for the different reactions necessary to confront the adversaries' actions. The fencing of the two adversaries made parades possible. It is thus that, in 1914, the encircling maneuvers of the Schlieffen plan or of the Marne could be avoided by a withdrawal or threatened by a counter-encirclement. Moreover, the rhythm of the maneuvers, because of the slowness of movements, allowed for reactions within manageable time.

With modern methods, traditional solutions became inapplicable because of the considerable increase of mobility. Here we come upon a new phenomenon which is the *absolute dissymmetry of the offensive and the defensive:* he who attacks possesses the initiative and, by a preconceived plan, he can develop a series of maneuvers without delay, while the defender who experiences the initiative of the adversary cannot react, even with great mobility, until he has a knowledge of the enemy's actions. At this point, the fencing of the opposing parties depends strictly on the *relationship of "agilities"* of the two adversaries.[1] The phenomenon that was noted in France in 1940 was reproduced on a larger scale in 1967 during the Six-Day War, where each of the three battles was found to be in fact decided from the first day. The result is that, under these conditions, ground combat becomes extremely unstable. After a long period in which battles had become progressively longer and longer, even as long as several months (Verdun, the Somme, Stalingrad) while at other times they had lasted only a few hours, we are coming back to a stage of evolution in which battles are becoming decisive in a few hours: let us say, one day.

This transformation imposes profound changes in our habits. To master the problem of the rapid decision battle, it is necessary to rediscover the recipes for great agility. It is certain that in today's land army we are encrusted with routines which are absolutely fatal: our habits of hierarchical transmission of information and orders are patently absurd. Moreover, the method of commanding with edited and typed operational orders no longer answers to needs, except in the offensive. In imitation of the navy and air force, the land army should relearn the means of maneuvering with the maximum agility possible. One should never again see battles in which, as in 1940, the Germans reacted in hours and the French in several days, and as in Sinai in 1967 when the Israelis reacted

---

[1] I call "agility" the combination of mobility and the reaction capacities: information, decision, transmission of orders, execution.

in a fraction of an hour and the Egyptians in days. It is a subject for a primary study which should be undertaken without delay and with the willingness to shake up all routines. The dividend could not fail to be considerably beneficial.

However, the improvement of agilities will not fully compensate for the disparity between the offensive and the defensive, unless by an improbable accident it should be the offensive which is starchy and the defensive which is agile. In the normal case of equal agilities, defense must bear the burden of reacting to adverse action *after* having detected it. It is this delay which gives the advantage to the offensive and which could be fatal to the defense. Only a great disparity of forces could compensate for this delay and we have seen by reason of the narrow limitation of forces because of the price of modern weapons that such differences of volume are quite difficult to imagine in favor of the defensive (that is to say, us), since at this moment the relationship between forces is unfavorable to the defense.

Fire power

The third factor, the estimated fire power of ground and air forces, can play a considerable role in battle.

This fire power, which modern weapons can make very dense and effective, is made up of two categories with very different characteristics:

1. *ground fire power* which can reach relatively short distances and which requires the deployment of land forces as well as logistic support in order to be concentrated, requiring delays (a function of "agility");

2. *air fire power* which, by reason of the speed and great range of action of airplanes or missiles, as well as aviation command procedures, can intervene quite rapidly and with considerable power and which, on open terrain, can have a formidable effectiveness.

Let us say then that *in conventional warfare, aviation is the weapon of powerful and mobile fire power.* It exercises an important influence on the battle because of this.

From this it can be said that the aerial situation becomes one of the important elements of the general situation. If one of the parties has total air superiority, and if its aerial forces are important, it can prevent the adversary from making any important concentrations and make daytime movements very difficult. Moreover, it can leisurely concentrate and deploy. It is this extreme situation which we have seen exploited by the Israelis as soon as they had put the Egyptian air force out of commission. It is this situation which justifies—and we will come back to it—the preliminary air battle in order to be assured of aerial superiority from the start. Land battle then becomes the exploitation of aerial victory.

If, on the other hand, the two opposing air forces, suitably equipped and protected, each possess a certain strength without one being able to quickly dominate the other, air fire power loses its predominance. It remains capable of intervening powerfully on ground forces operating ahead of the line of the adversary's interception, but it cannot stop movements taking place behind this interception line. Therefore, defensive ground operations rediscover a great efficacy, both on one side and the other. Operations tend to stabilize themselves, even if the front is weak and broken. This situation corresponds to that which could be observed in 1970 on the Suez Canal, beginning with the moment in which the Soviet ground-to-air missiles were deployed and completed by the presence of modern Soviet fighter units, making any Israeli penetration difficult and costly. In this case, the aerial situation entirely modifies the conditions of ground battle.

This conclusion, indisputable in the case of the Israeli-Egyptian War example, should be given nuances by the experiments made in Vietnam, where (on a different terrain, it is true, and in an unconventional war against guerrillas) the use of considerable aerial means revealed itself to be very deceiving. It is probable that the impact of the aerial situation can be reduced by appropriate combat procedures. It remains no less considerable in conventional warfare.

This is why the *principle of the preliminary aerial battle* remains very important. The Second World War had left procedures which the Israelis perfected in 1967 against an adversary who was a little sleepy and possibly misled by Soviet advisers: the surprise attack, outmaneuvering the radar of an air force which was practically unprotected and deployed too far forward, paid for itself with an almost instantaneous crushing blow. It was well played, but it is to be considered that, in the future, we will find few similar cases. The progress of radar and the means of aerial interception by aircraft, more echelonned and protected deployment and better planned alert measures should prevent surprise and the quick destruction of aerial forces. Starting from the moment when there will be no more surprise, the rate of attrition of opposing air forces will become very low and will limit itself to aerial combat, interception and to the rare surprising of airplanes on the ground. Under these conditions, aerial battle no longer tends to be rapidly decisive and even sinks into a prolonged confrontation with uncertain results. Naturally, in these conditions, this depends on the relationship between the opposing forces and their characteristic techniques. A large air force with a great reserve of pilots can accept a higher rate of attrition for the purpose of wearing away the enemy. A small air force of high quality, such as the Israeli Air Force, cannot offer itself the luxury of very costly aerial operations. On the whole, however, it could be thought that in our day, except in the case of serious negligence by one side (a hypothesis which is always possible), preliminary aerial battle in conventional warfare should not be quickly decisive and, consequently, could lead to a sort of aerial balance giving ground combat at least a part of the stability which it would lose due to the discontinuity of its forces and the greater mobility of the aggressor.

III. CONSEQUENCES FOR THE TACTICAL MANEUVER

From what we have just said about the influence of aerial forces, it follows that the maneuver in conventional warfare will be different depending on whether or not aerial superiority is obtained—or rather, which amounts to the same thing—whether the aerial factor is important or not.

If aerial superiority exists or has been obtained by one of the parties, he is in the process of developing a ground maneuver of decisive character. This is traditionally achieved by encirclement, preceded or not by a breakthrough maneuver. This was the plan of the campaign of France in 1940. There, the breakthrough was achieved by engaging tank concentrations with the support of air fire power against a continuous and static defensive front. The wide encirclement which followed was facilitated by the lack of mobility of the encircled forces, based on infantry and horse-drawn artillery and by the lack of agility in the French command. In 1967, the Israelis, in the presence of more modern forces, but discontinuous because of the extent of the operational theater, succeeded in dislodging in one day the defensive pivot which was made up of Egyptian infantry divisions by taking the defended areas from the flank, then by bringing most of their tanks against the rear of Egyptian armored divisions to fight them on a reversed front. In both cases, the ground support by the Israeli Air Force played a great part in the success of the maneuver. The battle thus takes a very rapidly decisive character, at least on the military level. It should be remembered that in the future, these profound actions on the rear will be carried out by aero-mobile operations made possible by aerial superiority.

This possibility confers a primary importance on the initial aerial battle and on the present formations in preparation for it. It is therefore essential that the air command be suitably divided in depth and protected, that the methods for alert be very vigilant, and that the interception systems, notably surface-to-air missiles, possess the protection and density to permit an assured effectiveness. It is this essentially aerial aspect of a tactical and technical nature which constitutes the strategic security of the whole. The fact should not be hidden that there still reign a number of false ideas in this area originating from practices of the Second World War and from intentions for using atomic weapons by the air force in expectation of preemptive action against enemy forces. The offensive deployment of NATO as well as of the Egyptians (under Soviet advice in 1967) proceeds from these relics, where logic has disappeared in conventional warfare.

We should now refer to other methods, capable of rendering a surprise air attack indecisive. This is a matter of life or death.

The case of aerial forces neutralizing each other

If air superiority cannot be obtained by either side when both air arms possess considerable capability, ground action becomes much more difficult. In this situation, an air force can fulfill two opposite functions: either crush the enemy's defenses at a given point in preparation for a breakthrough (an offensive role), or intervene forcefully against the adversary's ground attack (a defensive role). In both cases, ground support becomes the primary aviation mission as an air battle could not be quickly decisive.

Here again, methods of World War II (the caging-in of the battlefield, action against rear areas and industries) are to be very seriously modified: it is now a question of action on the *battlefield* and not of the progressive choking of the adversary. Moreover, in this situation of aerial nonsuperiority, it should be considered that the possibilities of the adversary's means of interception would narrowly limit the effectiveness of long-range actions. Similarly, aero-mobile operations can hardly be envisaged except in the immediate vicinity of the ground battlefield, even in the interior or at our rear.

Similarly, ground operations change character: more massive concentrations in full daylight and more movement outside of the zone of protection of friendly aviation. Dispersion, the use of night, the taking advantage of natural cover become the rule. It is not impossible to imagine that these methods allow for important tactical results, but the restraining action brought by the enemy air force can prevent the attainment of decisive strategic results. Battle would be joined by successive stages (as in 1918) or, in the case of deadlock, simply result in a sort of stabilization.

At this point, our interest is concentrated on the evolution of the aerial situation. In 1970 on the Suez Canal, we witnessed a very interesting aerial confrontation, because it did not constitute a true battle but a series of tests beginning with technical escalation destined to give warning of the probable results of a battle. It was, in this conventional sphere, a maneuver which was rather equivalent to what governs nuclear deterrence. It was a question of proving (to the Israelis) that the introduction of new material no longer permitted the deep penetrations which they had the habit of practicing as demonstrations. It could be observed, on this occasion, that in air war (as in strategic nuclear war) technical progress (more powerful surface-to-air missiles, faster interceptors) played an essential role. It is here that one can measure how much the conventional standard, already highly technical in its material (a modern airplane is worth its weight in gold) can increase only towards more elaborate techniques, and therefore come closer and closer in price to nuclear deterrence.

As a correlate, the volume of highly technical forces will have to be more and more restrained.

IV. STRATEGIC CONSEQUENCES

In the environment of total modern strategy which orders the limitation of conflicts, the strategy of conventional warfare is forced to obey specific and relatively new rules.

Strategy of "fait accompli"

Because of the reaction of world opinion against war in general (for fear of a nuclear escalation and because of a sort of allergy with regard to important political changes), it is essential that conventional warfare, if it is to succeed, should attain its political objectives in very short time periods (let us say a few days). It is therefore the dependable logic of the *strategy of the fait accompli* which, thanks to striking operations, modern technicians have made possible. This is what the Israelis accomplished with mastery in the Six-Day War, proving that we had thus entered into a new operational stage. Full motorization and aero-mobile actions have now become the *sine qua non* of a rapidly decisive war, the whole determined imperatively by the preliminary conquest of an almost absolute aerial superiority. Expeditionary corps operating far from their land bases draw their strength and effectiveness from airplane and helicopter carriers as well as from means of large amphibious landings. At a lesser distance, air transport—especially if it lands powerful enough equipment and sufficiently mobile equipment (light tanks), can play a decisive role in operations of a very limited objective, more or less in the form of *coups d'état* (such as the Germans accomplished in Norway in 1940). Let us say that, in general, such actions have a chance only in the presence of very inferior military adversaries, especially in the aerial sphere.

But the same Six-Day War also demonstrated that there existed a strong antidote to the strategy of the fait accompli. This strategy, already set in motion in Russia against Napoleon and by the initial victory of Hitler, has recourse to space, the withdrawal of the remaining forces, the maintenance of morale and the will to fight, in fact *the refusal to accept defeat* and the falling back of the strategic effort on the resources offered by modern total strategy. This is the appeal to international opinion, the search for foreign support. The reaction of Nasser after the Six-Day War was very effective in this sphere. In the end, conventional warfare aimed at breaking the will of the enemy by a military victory is without a decisive effect if that will refuses to allow itself to be defeated. This is the lesson of June 18, 1940 and, by contrast, the error committed in 1871 by the Government which called itself National Defense (Gambetta excluded).

Naturally, this strategy requires a larger space, a great deal of territory. In 1870, on the scale of the means of the period, France possessed that territory. In 1940, the Soviet or Chinese territory was necessary or recourse to world war applied this strategy. What makes the military victory of Israel in 1967 ineffective is the Arab space. An Arab victory over the Israelis would have completely different consequences. Let us say that *the strategy of the fait accompli by blitzkrieg is a strategy which is applicable only to small areas.* Moreover, as in everything which relates to limited warfare, it could not really succeed except for relatively unimportant political objectives.

Persuasive Strategy

If, on the contrary, the strategy of the fait accompli is revealed to be unattainable, either because the air force of the enemy has sufficient power or because the ground battle has not permitted the accomplishment of a decisive maneuver, the relative paralysis of the two adversaries then carries with it a slipping of strategy toward formulas in which the military conflict no longer plays any more than an auxiliary role within the complete context of *total strategy of a persuasive character.*

This is the great innovation due to the limited character of conflicts: at other times, the inability to attain a rapid military result led to the intensification of war, "the rise to extremes" according to Clausewitz. Today, this escalation is limited by its international context. Certainly, as soon as a stabilization of military operations is reached, the adversaries will seek exterior support: in Korea, this was China, and in the Middle East, the United States and the USSR. As during both of the two world wars, we witnessed a progressive extension of alliances to the point of giving the conflict a worldwide character. However, this extension became stabilized by the very fear of leading to a direct confrontation between the new allies. In Korea, it was the Yalu River (the Chinese frontier) that was to prevent a military decision. In the Middle East, the United States and the USSR intervened in order to maintain the balance, but also to maintain the conflict within the limits which they believed acceptable. The logic of the strategic situation, as in the military situation, is to impose a measured character on the conflict which forbids absolutely (or almost) all prospect of a military decision.

With this, war is pursued in a limited fashion with the objective of persuading the opposing countries to accept an *honorable compromise.* All of the resources of the total strategy are put into action to attain this result: limited military operations of a psychological character, international propaganda action, the intervention of the United Nations, political or economic pressures on governments, even *coups d'état* planned by special services of the allied powers in order to create governments which are more understanding, etc.

The result of this strategy is the opening of *negotiations:* interminable negotiations which can only reach their conclusion through the exhaustion of the belligerents. It is therefore necessary that the conflict last, that it be heavy enough to wear away the morale of the populations, that it be long enough to permit the evolution of ideas in support of a compromise judged unacceptable at first. The alternative to military victory (MacArthur said no such thing exists) is *protracted war* carried on and narrowly limited by international intervention.

V. ANALYSIS OF CONVENTIONAL WARFARE AGAINST GUERILLAS

This recourse to protracted war ends by closely connecting, through their strategy, traditional conventional warfare with warfare that is produced when conventional forces find themselves opposed against guerillas. This situation, which I studied at length in *La Guerre Révolutionnaire,* deserves to be analyzed here, at least in summary, in order to show its similarities and differences in relation to classic conventional warfare.

The fencing factor

Let us again take up the fencing factors of this warfare. *The volume and quality of the forces* in this case are completely asymmetrical. Conventional forces are powerful and mobile. They can conquer, occupy and defend any objective of their choice. The guerila forces are weak because of their weapons, which are generally portable; their mobility is that of the infantry. They are therefore incapable of combating the conventional forces in the open field or of chasing them from the positions they occupy. Because of this, the entire country can be traversed by conventional forces. Moreover, the latter benefit from the mobility of air transport as well as from powerful air-to-ground missiles. It seems, therefore, *a priori* that the match is too unequal in favor of the conventional forces.

As we know, especially since the Vietnamese War, this is not so. What is the cause then of this apparent contradiction?

The essential explanation of this contradiction is *the utilization of space by the guerillas.* In fact, in a situation of revolutionary warfare, the effective control of the terrain requires a considerable density of forces (let us say for example a battalion of 1,000 men for every 100 square kilometers, or 10 men to every square kilometer representing a bare minimum). Therefore, the conventional forces are never numerous enough to control the entire territory (3 million men would be necessary to control Vietnam, 5 million to control France). With manpower necessarily more limited in an expeditionary corps, only a tenth or a twentieth of the terrain is effectively occupied. By systematically refusing to engage and by taking refuge in unoccupied zones, the guerillas find it possible to survive, to live off the population and to carry on surprise actions in order to profit from favorable opportunities. In this way, they are able to maintain a psychological pressure on the occupiers and keep their prestige up before the world.

This guerilla tactic, on the basis of dispersion and mobility, is made even more indispensable by the power of air fire power. In Vietnam, the American air force has dropped millions of tons of bombs which could not be dodged except by an extreme dispersion combined with a very rapid and almost systematic concealment and protection by digging in. We come here to a second major asymmetry: the conventional forces can concentrate—they must, in fact, in order not to give the guerillas any hold—while the guerilla forces are widely dispersed, being able to operate their units only by surprise and for a very short time.

Consequences for the tactical maneuver

In this situation, one side can exploit the conventional tactical capacity of his forces if he meets the enemy and knows how to engage him. The whole tactic of the regular forces therefore rests on information and the mobility which permits taking advantage of that information. Experience has shown that, from the time when the information ceases to be current and very exact, conventional operations become self-deceiving. Moreover, taking advantage of information, even if it is excellent, is very difficult. One must move rapidly, conduct a sufficiently large encirclement by surprise, then mop up the area very thoroughly. Even with parachutists and helicopters, it is very difficult, especially if the terrain is wooded or mountainous. In the face of an alert guerilla, search and destroy missions are hazardous.

Another solution has been tried, founded on the relative bulk of guerilla logistics. The latter, fed by gangs of coolies, cannot operate in poor areas except from bases where their munitions and rations are located. By attaching themselves to these bases, necessarily in fixed locations, the guerillas can be forced to fight when the bases are known or else the bases can be destroyed, thus disorganizing their possible activities. The Americans have used this tactic quite often—which we inaugurated in Tonkin in 1947—with success. It has sometimes produced interesting results, but it has never been known to be decisive.

From the guerilla point of view, tactical procedures are determined by the situation. If the regular forces are very concentrated and very active, the guerillas cannot subsist except by dividing into very small units, sometimes two to five men, while, at the same time, holding the population in obedience through a merciless terror, to prevent them from informing the enemy. In extremity, the resistance acts completely in secret, hiding arms and dressing in civilian clothing, because the essential element for them is to survive and maintain their influence on the population. This situation has occurred several times, especially in Algeria and in Vietnam. In this case, the regular forces and the guerillas completely overlap. The guerillas then limit their action to terrorism against the population, to propaganda and a few attempts which are more or less fireworks to maintain their prestige.

If, on the contrary, the regular forces are less concentrated and less watchful, guerillas can organize and live in small units (platoons, companies) located in dens from which they emerge to carry out ambushes or surprise attacks based on information furnished by secret networks maintained in the zone occupied by regular troops. These small operations do not aim at obtaining important military results but at harassing the regulars and especially at striking the imagination of the population. It is military action with psychological intentions.

If, finally, regular forces are not very numerous and passive, guerilla forces, with the logistic support of sympathetic foreigners, can form real combat units (battalions, regiments and even divisions) and then carry on what I have termed "la grande guerilla". It is an operation in which major units apply guerilla methods (dispersion, secrecy and surprise) to important engagements with the enemy. In this form of warfare, important tactical results can be obtained against regular forces (the destruction of the Charton column on RC #4 in 1950, the taking of Langson, the siege and capture of Dien Bien Phu to cite only examples taken from the Indochina war). In Vietnam, we have witnessed large American units, having the advantage of strong air support, held in check by Vietnamese forces. We ourselves had to take on—and moreover win—a veritable battle at Vinh Yen against two North Vietnamese divisions in Tonkin in 1951 which had set up an enormous ambush with guerilla procedures.

What characterizes all of these forms of guerilla warfare are their tactics of mobility by secrecy and surprise, the absolute absence of any fixed front, their violence and boldness in a state of marked superiority and systematic withdrawal when that superiority is lacking. It is the rational application of the maxims which Mao Tse-tung has drawn from his experiences against the Japanese and the Nationalists. They make up the entire strength of guerilla warfare. If, on the contrary, guerillas are attempting to establish strongholds (as did the OAS in 1961) or are still strangers to the local population and are grouped in well-separated camps (such as the Feddayin Palestinians in Jordan), they are easily crushed. It is the same when the support of the population is insufficient, either because its resources are too weak or because political action has not been pressed vigorously (such as in South America with the rural guerillas). On the other hand guerilla warfare possesses a great capacity for psychological action on the level of urban terrorism through assassination or spectacular hijackings.

Strategic consequences

The basic character of all of these tactics is to allow, at best, only partial and local successes, except for the extreme cases in which one of the adversaries reaches the point of moral collapse (such as in the victory of the Communists in China). Under normal conditions, the type of warfare in which regular forces are opposed to guerillas is usually indecisive. It is a *protracted war* in which military actions are part of a *total strategy of a persuasive character* aiming essentially to lead to the weariness of the adversary.

This is to say that, even more than in prolonged conventional wars, psychological factors as well as the economic and diplomatic factors will play a major role. For both sides, it will be a question of mobilizing sympathies, obtaining material and moral support, of wearing away the will of the adversary and undermining the cohesion of national opinions. Thus, an *exterior maneuver* is developed outside the war zone and on the world chessboard which will definitely be the essential element of the final decision. This decision will come, according to the now familiar pattern, after a long *phase of negotiations* towards the form of a more or less honorable compromise.

From the military point of view, the exterior maneuver could play a considerable role by permitting the existence of bases at the borders of the war zone, invulnerable because of political constraints. Such were the Chinese bases near Tonkin, as were the Tunisian and Moroccan bases near Algeria, as were the Cambodian and Laotian bases near South Vietnam which permitted operations to continue during those wars, while they materialized in the eyes of the population the exterior supports which were allowed them. This was a powerful moral factor which, in Algeria for example, succeeded in compensating psychologically for the defeat of the internal guerilla movement. On the other hand, guerillas which found themselves geographically isolated (Mau-Mau, Malaysia, the Palestinian Feddayins) were unable to endure for very long.

Evidently, the key to the survival of guerilla warfare is that the population be capable without weakening of withstanding the danger and destruction which the guerillas bring them. To keep the morale of the population at the desired height, it is necessary that the guerillas depend upon a *political line* which has been very well conceived in relation to the latent desires of the people (independence, patriotism, xenophobia, political ideology). This is the reason why guerilla warfare is hardly ever employed outside of *revolutionary warfare* or *wars of liberation.*

On the level of the interior maneuver taking place within the war zone, there exists a particular military strategy which has been equally misunderstood in the context of the different historic examples at our disposal. For guerilla warfare, it is a question of *menacing the adversary over the largest possible area,* a strategy which Lawrence explained magnificently in *The Seven Pillars of Wisdom* with respect to the Medina campaign. Doing so, it obliges regular forces to disperse their means over an area exceeding their capability, while the guerillas remain capable of acting wherever they choose. It is thus that 10,000 to 20,000 Algerian fellagahs held 400,000 French troops at bay and that 1,000,000 South Vietnamese and 500,000 Americans were not able to finish off some 200,000 adversaries. By the same token, the regular forces must know how to practice a very delicate strategy consisting of knowing how to choose areas whose political importance justifies their strict control, and how to maintain a series of operations throughout the rest of the country to prevent the guerillas from developing their forces and digging in. It is the correct proportion of these two activities which permits military forces to obtain their greatest effectiveness; without, however, obtaining a decision. From this point of view, it appears incontestable that the French forces in Algeria were progressively too dispersed and that the purpose for the extension of the operational theatre and therefore of the regular forces is to oblige the enemy to undertake a prolonged, major military effort, which contributes to accelerating the process of eroding public opinion.

It is quite remarkable to note that, in the course of the history of colonial wars, guerilla warfare could never be defeated except by very long operations and by acting more and more like a drop of oil spreading progressively. The pacification of Algeria lasted almost 40 years, that of Indochina 30 years, that of Morocco 27 years. Such durations were possible only because the expeditionary forces were very limited, but there was wide participation of locally recruited forces among the partisans of the occupier. Because of this, the colonial war became a civil war with very limited foreign participation. A large military effort is necessarily short in duration. Today moreover, the power of modern means of communication of news would not permit keeping world opinion in ignorance. The fatality of modern war with conventional forces in combat with guerillas is that it is long but relatively limited in time (Indochina seven years, Algeria seven years, Vietnam seven years) and that they end by a compromise after interminable diplomatic exchanges. Otherwise, the guerillas make a certain number of mistakes and they are rapidly crushed (Jordan). However, the general effectiveness of guerilla warfare is such that it can always be seen to rise again when political or racial tensions are sufficient.

In any case, the military operations of the party that plays the guerilla dispersion game will serve only to gain time, alert world opinion and serve as a political argument for the benefit of an appropriate total strategy. The decision will then result either from the weariness of the exploited adversary because of outside pressures (Algeria) or from the military results obtained by a strong ally (Liberation).

VI. CONCLUSIONS

Reflection on conventional warfare, clarified by so many recent examples, demonstrates how much this form of warfare has changed its character and what new and complex rules govern it. The first conclusion clearly indicates that the subject must be completely relearned by eliminating the methods which we were used to. In the aerial sphere, as well as in the ground arena, a new understanding has become necessary because the perpetuation of ancient rules would be very dangerous. Similarly, conscious distinction between tactical analysis and strategic analysis is completely evident. The liaison between these two points of view, operational analysis, becomes essential.

Among the crowd of new ideas which appear, I will retain in my conclusion only three important ideas which I believe to be primary.

1. The first, which we encountered without entering into an analysis of the relative function of the volume and the quality of the military forces, is the distinction between conventional forces with highly technological qualifications, which are rare and costly, and primitive forces of little expense which can be multiplied at will.

We meet here, at the level of conventional warfare, the same subdivision in *technical levels* which we encountered at the level of strategic nuclear deterrence. By analogy with the classification which we already outlined of the levels "0" and "1", we will call the level of conventional forces of high technical complexity *"level 2"* and the level of inexpensive primitive force *"level 3"*. By the same logic that moves level 1 to meet level 0, it is evident that technical evolution will move level 2 to meet the technical complexity of level 1. In other words, it will become more and more expensive and difficult for nations of average size to keep up-to-date, unless in the form of examples stripped of all tactical and strategic significance.

This consideration leads us to the maxim that *on the national level, the future rests on "level 3"* provided its role is foreseen according to its worth and the measure of the morale of the nation. This conclusion is very important and normally leads to the concept sooner or later of the existence of conventional forces combining levels 2 and 3 in logical and harmonious fashion.

2. This conclusion becomes all the more evident when we note that traditional conventional warfare—that is, between forces at "level 2"—has become terribly unstable by virtue of reduction of armed forces, their great mobility and their firepower, particularly in the aerial sphere. This instability is very dangerous because it can lead to the temptation of *the strategy of the fait accompli*. It

is the return of military adventurism at a time when errors in calculation are repaid with considerable dangers.

We have now seen that the precondition of the strategy of the fait accompli was a favorable aerial situation. As well as the antidote to the fait accompli is the existence of a defensive air force possessing both a considerable firepower and important survival capacities. Such an air force can make a rapidly decisive conventional battle impossible and force the war to move into a persuasive strategy. *We would have, at this point, a process of deterrence of conventional warfare towards the fait accompli.* However, the difficulty of this method is that it requires an aerial situation which would be about equal between the two adversaries, that is to say a race for air forces essentially at "level 2", which the smaller and weaker would have difficulty in maintaining. If the aggressor possesses a certain superiority in the air from the start, the chances of the defender knowing how to impose a long war and a persuasive strategy are very limited. In the present situation of the NATO forces, for example, it is clear that this deterrence by conventional air forces is inoperative and that, *in order to come to a sufficient stability at the conventional level, a special deterrence has become absolutely indispensable.*

3. In the sphere of conventional warfare, *the only existing deterrent is that of the guerilla.* The different experiences of confrontation between regular forces and guerilla forces have been sufficiently deceiving so as to render the prospect of coming up against a generalized guerilla as sufficient to discourage aggression. China and Yugoslavia have played with this deterrent strategy with some results. However, such a strategy is not *credible* unless the necessary preconditions are all present: large geographic area, difficult terrain, a tough and determined population and widespread political and patriotic feeling throughout the country. It would be very unrealistic to say that, in the present situation, the necessary preconditions are all present in Western Europe. Certainly, we can hope to be able to use guerilla methods, but this prospect at the beginning of a war is too uncertain to have it constitute a valid deterrence.

4. At this point, if we aim to confer on conventional warfare the stability which it has lost in our day, it is indispensable that we have recourse to other means.

This will be the subject of the next chapter.

Chapter IV

THE LEVEL OF
TACTICAL NUCLEAR DETERRENCE

I. DISCUSSION OF TACTICAL NUCLEAR WEAPONS

Atomic weapons described as "tactical" date from the beginning of the 1950's. They preceded thermonuclear weapons. Their history—with some differences—is analogous to that of weapons described as "strategic."

During their initial acceptance, so-called "tactical" atomic weapons were less powerful nuclear weapons, designed to be used on the battlefield, somewhat like heavy artillery. In the beginning, this was in fact a plane-carried bomb, shortly afterwards it was a nuclear warhead of a short range missile (Honest John, Corporal, Sergeant, etc.) then, later, one of longer range (Pershing), until the miniaturization of warheads permitted it to be made into the shell of heavy artillery (240, then 155) and into a mortar shell (Davy Crockett). All these devices—and their counterparts in the Soviet Army—exist simultaneously and constitute a complete panoply of very different and very numerous weapons (it is said 7,000 of them on the American side within Europe) and, in general, it is undecided how they are to be used. For once, the arsenal has preceded the concept (this is also what happened for strategic nuclear weapons) or rather the initial conflict transformed itself more quickly than the arsenal constituted successive generations.

Moreover, we have used aerial terminology to speak of tactics and strategy, but when thermonuclear weapons appeared, they did not lack for theoreticians to maintain that this superpowerful weapon might have a tactical use. After all, the 20 kiloton Hiroshima bomb had had a "strategic" use. In fact, there exists today a complete array of nuclear arms, from the Davy Crockett of a fraction of a kiloton to the thermonuclear weapon of several tens of megatons, including nuclear mines, shells, ballistic and flying missiles and bombs. The problem—somewhat poorly resolved—is to know what to do with this panoply.

Characteristics of tactical nuclear weapons

In order to try to clarify the problem, let us first analyze the characteristics of the "tactical" nuclear weapon.

If the criterion is use on the battlefield, these are "counter-force" arms, destined to destroy or neutralize the opposing forces (nuclear, air force, land forces) and to thus facilitate the action of our own forces. From this comes the idea of seeking arms of restrained power in order to act against the enemy without hitting friendly troops and in order to spare, as much as possible, the civilian population. In summary, the "tactical" atomic arm would be, above all, a selective weapon—which applies rather poorly to thermonuclear devices. It would tend, to a certain degree, to humanize nuclear war.

In spite of this relatively reassuring characteristic, it represents an escalation of absolutely extraordinary violence: an average atomic weapon of 20 kilotons produces an explosive force equivalent to that of a salvo of four million 75 mm cannons, a concentration of artillery never dreamed of in the past. As I have written in *L'Introduction à la Stratégie* "this enormous power, whose effectiveness is still further multiplied by atomic fallout, is released and positioned by only a few men. It is an extraordinary revolution."

Moreover, this crushing firepower possesses a nearly total mobility, thanks to the various means of launching. This contrasts with the heaviness of the mass armies of yesterday in which it was necessary to concentrate 1,000 airplanes in order to destroy Hamburg and all the cannons of an army in order to destroy Berlin.

Let us stop here for a moment: the extreme innovation of the atomic weapon is the mobility of the powerful bombs. *There is no longer a relation between power and mass*—at least in the first analysis. Thus, we would have in this (it has been believed) the ultimate weapon.

Unfortunately, in the tactical field as in the strategic field, the essential problem resides in that fact that *the two adversaries possess like weapons* and it is not possible to be completely protected from them. In fact, the question of protection has naturally been studied with care and the results are very disappointing. The interception of tactical weapons (whose trajectory is short) is very difficult and of a very weak efficiency. Physical protection, because of the technical characteristics of the explosions, has only a statistical efficiency: by going underground or the use of armor, one reduces the danger zone from explosive action, but near point zero (proximity of which can vary from 500 meters for 20 kilotons to several kilometers for megatons) there is no chance for survival. One then has recourse to *dispersion* (which has been a constant solution throughout the development of the power of firearms) which has the effect of reducing the efficiency of the bombs, but which also has the result of bringing the tactical effectiveness of conventional forces to nearly zero without preventing the risk of rapid and unacceptable attrition rates.

Consequently, we no longer know very well how to use the ultimate weapon . . .

II. ATTEMPTS IN THE DIRECTION OF A CONCEPT FOR THE USE OF TACTICAL NUCLEAR WEAPONS

The American technicians, who ruled over conceptualization in matters of atomic warfare during the 1950's, had invented rational formulas which were completely inapplicable to war: it was necessary to use these weapons on "paying objectives," thus one had to seek out enemy "concentrations," photograph them and have these photographs examined by atomic experts who then judged if the objective was worth the expense. In spite of modern communication, this procedure required several hours and when the weapon was "delivered," it was quite possible that the "paying objective" had disappeared.

Increasing the cost of this tactic of releasing bombs, the American and British tacticians estimated that the defense could "channel the opposing forces" into spaces in order to "force them to be concentrated" so that they would become paying objectives.

I mention these futile notions here only in order to show how much the extraordinary technical progress had disoriented a military thought of an incredible weakness. At the same time, they proclaimed "the atomic weapon is a weapon like others but more powerful; it changes nothing in the principles of war." Let us note in passing that the Soviets were making analogous comments at the same time.

Rather quickly (between five and ten years) it became necessary to look at the facts: resistance moles which were supposed to channel the enemy would be destroyed by atomization and this enemy (if he were not stupid and possessed the appropriate tactics) would *never* be concentrated.

Moreover, they proceeded to a multitude of exercises on the map (I myself began at the head of the Interallied Tactical Study Group in 1952) and later on the ground. At the beginning, they started on the premise that the atomic weapon would be scarce and expensive, but they very quickly (1953) began to envisage the case in which the atomic weapon would be very abundant and used without limitation by both sides.

They then discovered a host of new problems. First of all, any fixed, dense resistance would be destroyed at the end of several hours, at the latest. Defensive tactics had to change in nature and it was thought that the only solution, consequently, in our defensive attitude was to act by counter-attack using atomic explosions. The result was that only a "mobile defense" was possible, one which was very dispersed in order to reduce losses, composed of armored units in order to use permanent (but relatively) organic protection, at the same time having a mobility allowing for the elasticity of the dispersal maneuver. However, if both parties were dispersed, there would no longer be any "paying objectives" according to the preceding thesis. The rate of dispersion separating the different units to a distance from the danger zone of average atomic weapons—too long fixed at the battalion echelon by rule of thumb—was evidently at the company echelon at the minimum, this being the smallest unit capable of having cohesion and the necessary polyvalency. Consequently, the calculation of losses from weapons of weak power (10 to 20 kilotons) became a statistical affair. Calculation, like the map exercises and war games, showed that attrition would be relatively modest (200 men for 20 kilotons; 10 per kiloton!) if dispersion tactics were well respected. However, in this dispersion, would it not be possible to use new conventional procedures (infiltration, ambush) derived from a sort of mechanized guerilla warfare? Finally, would not the bomb-proof counter-attack, panacea of those who nostagically remember Rommel and Guderian, have the effect of very quickly attracting atomic response? It would be necessary to know how to put very alert tactics—from which we are rather far—into practice with very problematical chances for success.

This was very risky also, because it was quite difficult to imagine all the possible reactions of troops to atomic fire. Certainly, protection and dispersion would reduce losses, but what would be the psychological effect of these explosions which would, in a matter of seconds, burn everything in a radius of three kilometers, blow up trees and houses, transform villages into burned ruins and forests into clearings? Would the fear of mysterious radiations not terrorize the troops? Could control over the battle be maintained after several explosions?

They were then tempted to take action upon the enemy rear, to profit from the power of the weapons to rapidly crush enemy aviation on his own ground, destroy enemy depots and their logistical possibilities when required, by using more powerful weapons. However, the enemy could do the same and they could only expect generalized disorder.

Finally, two formidable obstacles were encountered. The first is that the rate of military dispersion recognized as necessary was far higher than that of the civilian population, especially in West Germany. So much so that statistical civilian loss, calculated by the square kilometer, far exceeded military loss (20 military losses on the average per square kilometer, and 100 to 150 civilian). Naturally, the large metropolitan areas and cities posed insoluble problems because the density there is considerable.

The second obstacle, which has been put forth sometimes with a bit of exaggeration—especially by sentimental opponents of nuclear weapons—is that of the general contamination of the atmosphere because of the long life span of certain radioactive pollutions and their progressive distribution into the stratosphere. Existing weapons produced these pollutions in rather large quantities; there was danger for all of humanity if a certain number of explosions were exceeded and this number was rather low. Attempts were made to produce less "dirty" bombs which would be almost "clean". Prospects exist in this direction which have not yet been fully exploited.

The American solution of 1957 and its consequences

Faced with this mountain of problems and contradictions, it was necessary to draw up a doctrine. In 1957, at the time when it seemed necessary to reinforce the defensive capacity of NATO troops to permit delay of the unleashing of massive retaliation, the American doctrine chose an operational strategy based on *mobile defense,* with local counter-attacks by dispersed troops, whereas the enemy would be subjected to a considerable attrition rate by in-depth fire. According to this conception, the tactical atomic weapon played the role of a multiplier of the power of conventional forces, on the condition that the latter applied appropriate tactics.

The many exercises and maneuvers which were then performed using two adversaries with analogous tactics showed that the attrition of conventional forces was so rapid that several days (and several thousand atomic weapons) were sufficient to reduce the existing forces to zero. This strategy did not present very great credibility, but *precisely because of the unsoluble problems that it posed to the two parties,* it possessed a *great deterrent value.* Because of this, more than for its rather doubtful operational value, it was taken as official doctrine of NATO.

When Kennedy was elected in 1960, the great preoccupation of his brain trust was to avoid accidental war (through error) and, consequently, the spontaneous escalation and its reflections allowed them to carry out—for a time—a very powerful and very stable strategic deterrence. Under these conditions, the arsenal of tactical atomic weapons became both superfluous and dangerous. The first reflex was to carry this whole arsenal to the rear and to curb it by a complete security system. Some would have abolished it purely and simply, but the existence of this arsenal constituted a more and more powerful political argument in proportion to the diminishing credibility of strategic nuclear deterrence. McNamara himself often noted this, but without revealing that the rules for using these weapons were radically changed because they would not be used, if they ever were, except after a conventional battle in which the will of the enemy would be tested. Under these conditions, the deterring capacity of these weapons was carried to a second possible phase which well could never be used unless the first phase, instead of being a retarding action, was transformed into a rout. They could be usable only if our side had a second echelon of forces of a sufficient volume at their disposal, which they did not. The gap in deterrence, which they had wanted to plug up in 1957, was now wide.

The Soviet solution of 1960 (?)

This is without a doubt what incited the Soviets to choose a completely different strategy, carefully conceived with a view towards putting the American solution on the wrong tack—which is good warfare.

Since the key to the new war was survival, and defensive tactics had lost all value, the Soviets decided on the necessity of offensive and strategic tactics. Thanks to this, through an increased mobility, one could penetrate deeply into opposing dispositions, disorganize its reactions, mix with its troops and civilian populations and in this way effectively protect itself from tactical atomic responses. In addition, the victory would cause a snow-ball effect. The initial crushing of the conventional forces, coupled with the threat of strategic bombardments, would be sufficient to cause a moral shock great enough to bring about a political decision—at first limited, if necessary. This was a modernized formula of the blitzkrieg of 1940, but with the use of atomic explosions. In this area, Sokolowski's book does not for a moment seem to put in doubt the possibility of using atomic explosions which can be anti-forces and selective, carried out by rapid mechanized or airborne operations. On the other hand, these procedures for offensive combat aiming at outclassing the enemy by superior agility, can, through brief concentrations, destroy by swift action dispersed conventional troops in the conventional phase. Moreover, the recognized existence of this preliminary phase can encourage exploitation to easily win the battle of the frontiers, a victory which can bring about the collapse of the enemy morale.

This body of very homogeneous concepts is not without flaws. Its eventual value rests on the postulate that the enemy (NATO) will be dispersed, not alert, and slow to unleash its atomic bombs. This is not necessarily true and, in case of error, this frenzied offensive strategy may be transformed into a catastrophe.

In addition, such military methods do not absolutely correspond to the present political atmosphere in Europe. They doubtless have only an academic value, but it must be recognized that Soviet military thought is being oriented in a more logical direction than official current American military thought because they are both hypothetically effective and surely deterrent.

In any case, it currently appears that the Soviet offensive doctrine requires a serious adjustment of our conceptions concerning tactical atomic weapons. We must draw up a well-adapted alternative doctrine to face this one, capable of restoring the deterrence established in 1957 and which has become necessary at the tactical level, now that strategic nuclear deterrence is losing its power of extended deterrence for the benefit of other levels and of Europe.

III. THE DETERRENT EXPLOITATION OF TACTICAL ATOMIC WEAPONS

For lack of the power to insure that the use of tactical atomic weapons would bring about the defeat of the enemy—which would be the best deterrence, but we have seen that it is hardly credible—deterrence by atomic weapons can be founded on only three concepts:

1. the certainty, or at least the very great probability, that these weapons would be used very soon in case of aggression;

2. the uncertainty of the psychological consequences of their use;

3. the uncertainty of the development of operations during which tactical atomic weapons would be used.

In addition, it is absolutely essential to anticipate, through appropriate arrangements, offensive enemy tactics in order to deny all their immediate effectiveness.

*Re-establishment of the probability of the use of
tactical atomic weapons*

In order to create the certainty of the use of tactical atomic weapons in case of invasion, we can use three categories of procedure. The first is of a declaratory nature. It is currently used, but with nuances (due to the theory of flexible response) which remove a good part of its credibility, especially at the beginning of the aggression. The reason for this ambiguity is explained by the American desire not to engage the decision of the President, a legitimate preoccupation, but one which could in no way prevent a clearer declaration of principle, while reserving the effective decision for the moment of possible conflict. It is explained also by the fear of worrying German public opinion, which is very concerned (and justly so) with not becoming a nuclear battle field.

The second procedure consists of demonstrating this desire by exercises and maneuvers, in sum, by publicity given to a doctrine of use which is sufficiently well conceived (not the case at present) in order to convince the enemy of the risk of seeing tactical atomic weapons used quickly, in any case before conventional forces are seriously engaged, thus possibly compromised. By caricaturing a bit, this would come back to renouncing the initial phase of conventional defense or at least reducing to a minimum the existence of this phase.

The third procedure rests on starting technical research on production of tactical atomic weapons which are sufficiently "clean" for use in adequate quantities without causing unacceptable pollution and even to reduce destruction on the battlefield. Such research, followed by projects which are put into effect, would constitute deterrent proof to a great degree.

Developing uncertainty on the psychological
consequences of tactical atomic weapons

Sokolowski's book generously depicts a "rocket war" which, for those who have seriously studied the problem, contains optimism on the possibilities of carrying out such operations and which, above all, entirely neglects the psychological impact of nuclear explosions on troops. As we have already said above, this conception can only truly stand up if one starts from the premise that this offensive will not meet a determined and alert adversary and that atomic weapons will be used too late, after contact with the enemy troops has been accomplished. It is thus indispensable to cast doubt on the possibility of carrying out such a maneuver (a question of tactics and operational strategy) and to make a generalized use of atomic weapons feared by pointing out consequences it could not help but have on troop morale. Let us not forget what the revelation of modern arms was on the battlefield at Saint Privat in 1870 and especially in 1914. This is an aspect which must be explored, not to demoralize our own troops, but to avoid dangerous illusions in the minds of our adversaries. Moreover, all things being equal, Sokolowski's doctrine is even more unrealistic than the doctrine of Colonel Grandmaison in 1914. Despite this, the mad bayonet offensive did perform miracles in Italy against a passive adversary. The Prussian offensive of 1870, based on initiative and outflanking the enemy, easily defeated the fixed defense of the French. Extrapolation from the time of the machine gun, rapid fire cannon and smokeless powder was revealed to be catastrophic despite the above examples. It is probable that we are witnessing an analogous phenomenon today, but a greatly amplified one. One must note this and demonstrate it by perfecting procedures for the use of tactical nuclear weapons to procure great agility with atomic bombs.

So, the possibility opened by Soviet offensive doctrine seems to be full of hazards. Deterrence will be restored from it.

Developing the uncertainty of the possibility of
conducting such operations with tactical nuclear weapons

The same line of thought must allow for developing a serious uncertainty over the possibility of conducting such operations with the use of tactical atomic weapons. Of course, first of all, there is the power and mobility of the bombs. However, there is also uncertainty concerning the efficiency of radio communications from the moment that ion explosions are produced in the troposphere and the prospect of situations changing extremely, as much on the front as in the rear. From experience at the beginnings of wars, it is not difficult to imagine disorders of all types happening: movement of populations, false news and alarms; the terror of the paratroops, of the fifth column, of the civilian population because of nuclear fallout. *The initial scenario cannot help but be disturbed.* The probability, after a phase of disordered opposition, is for a kind of dispersed, underground stabilization, turning to a kind of guerilla warfare at the forward posts while the civilian population, in a stupor, demands the opening of negotiations. This tableau is probable, *on condition that* things do not happen as in 1940 in France, when the unforeseen blitzkrieg constantly outclassed the defense.

To avoid this possibility—the only one which would justify confidence in the offensive maneuver—it is thus necessary to fulfill a certain number of tactical, operational, and strategic conditions which constitute the key to deterrence.

IV. CONDITIONS FOR A BASIC DETERRENT ACTION OF TACTICAL ATOMIC WEAPONS

Deterrence at the tactical nuclear level does not consist of predicting and preparing for a battle with tactical nuclear weapons, a battle which in any case would be both an adventure and a catastrophe. *Deterrence consists of preventing such a battle from taking place* by an ensemble of appropriate provisions.

Tactical conditions

On the tactical plane, it is essential to show the possible adversary that his maneuver risks failure by improving the agility of the conventional forces substantially, as well as by the mobility and speed of releasing tactical nuclear fire bombs. These improvements, besides being completely urgent, are to be emphasized in exercises, maneuvers and documents. This is essentially a relatively easy task if we know how to apply ourselves to it. The goal to be reached is attaining a practical maneuverability superior to that which the Soviets show in their maneuvers. It is, at the same time, an affair of communications, less routine methods of control to be instituted, and increased mobility.

Thus, the realization of the alert tool, whose military command needs to be capable of baffling the enemy offensive maneuver, would be accomplished.

Operational conditions

On the operational plane, three problems must be resolved: preventing a decision which might happen in the initial phase before possibly opening nuclear fire; deciding hypothetical conditions for releasing tactical atomic fire; and deciding on dispositions of conventional forces at the time of releasing atomic fire.

To prevent a decision which might result from the initial phase before possibly opening tactical atomic fire, it is essential—vital—*to avoid from the beginning* conventional defensive battle as now conceived. Such a result can only be achieved by replacing advance troops as they now exist by an extremely light mobile screen, meant to delay the enemy advance at a sufficient depth to obtain the time lag needed for proper deployment of defensive forces. The grave danger of being broken through and enveloped by the enemy forces, resulting in entanglement with the enemy which subsequently prevents any use of tactical atomic weapons, is thus avoided. This requires having sufficient available depth, which poses a political problem.

The conception of the possible release of tactical nuclear weapons must stem from the idea that the tactical atomic weapon is, above all, a psychological means whose possible use must disturb the enemy's offensive plan and introduce total uncertainty as to the results of operations into the enemy's planning. Indeed, it must always be considered that atomic tactical weapons have never been used and that it is impossible to predict the reactions of troops who will be submitted to these explosions. Moreover, it is not impossible that the result would be a complete collapse of morale, perhaps even between both adversaries. For all these reasons, *the opening of nuclear fire would represent a crucial moment in the battle,* a unique occasion which perhaps will never again occur; especially one that *we must not let the enemy exploit.* Thus, it is necessary:

1. to reserve for ourselves the hypothetical priority to the use of tactical nuclear fire should the enemy attack in a conventional way;

2. *to use these weapons in such a way as to draw the maximum dividends from them.*

The first consideration completely forbids any concept of "warning shots" which would allow the enemy to take the initiative in the general use of nuclear weapons in good conscience relative to international opinion.

The second consideration leads first to envisage an opening of atomic fire which, if not massive, is at least *generalized* and *simultaneous* so that the majority of the enemy units see nuclear explosions and, on the other hand, so that the effect of the explosions is exploited by deep counter-attacks designed to instill panic in the enemy. What is necessary is a *counter-offensive counter-thrust.* We do not know if this would be possible but it is the only preconceived attitude which can give our troops a high enough morale under these difficult circumstances. It must also be recognized that the enemy could counter rather quickly and that it is highly desirable to have accomplished a mixing-up with enemy troops at this time. This would be the best protection as long as we had the initiative. Nuclear weapons should thus be foreseen as preparation and accompaniment for counter-attacks conceived to be both disorganizing and deep (20, 50, 100 km).

Strategic conditions

The predictions for use of tactical nuclear weapons have, in reality, no tactical incidence: *it is not in any way a question of fighting a tactical atomic battle, but on the contrary of making this impossible* by the accomplishment of a highly deterrent attitude. In sum, *it is, at the tactical level, the absolute equivalent of what is accomplished at the strategic level.*

However, as at the strategic nuclear level, it is absolutely essential to bring into play a *strategy tending to reinforce the credibility of the tactical deterrent threat,* which ultimately results in restoring a sufficient degree of credibility to total deterrence.

The declared, visibly organized forecast of a generalized use of tactical atomic weapons removes any stray impulse from the enemy to seek a local decision through conventional battle. He knows he is taking great risks and that he will not avoid a form of limited nuclear confrontation, denying him all hope of being able to unfold his plan and hope for an easy success.

The greatest strategic interest in deterrence by tactical atomic weapons is to be situated at an intermediary echelon, dominated by deterrent strategic weapons. For that reason, *the risk* of escalation is very weak because of the stability of the nuclear strategic level, while the *credibility* of a tactical nuclear response remains very great because of its localization and its possible operational effectiveness.

However, this credibility must be reinforced in the strategic domain by the following measures:

1. *Regarding civilians,* rightly concerned by preparations for an atomic battle, it is essential to make them understand that the announcement of possible use of nuclear strategic weapons has the effect of preventing aggression and thus the battle which they fear. The risks of such an announcement are largely balanced by its deterrent character. On the other hand, these risks for the population can be largely reduced by the preliminary evacuation of civilians from front-line areas and by construction of light shelters, both of which are possible in short time periods. Also, an action of this kind and its preparation,

showing that one means to apply this strategy, would have considerable deterrent effect.

2. We have seen that avoiding conventional battle, just as regrouping forces before a counter-offensive, would require a certain depth of available terrain. This necessity seems unacceptable to the Germans who must worry about not giving up one inch of national territory without fighting. The "forward strategy" can constitute a true suicide as we have seen in France in 1940 and in Egypt in 1967. No political reason can justify such a strategy if it is dangerous from the military point of view. But above all, since it is not a matter of strategy of action, it is a battle for which one rightly prepares in order to avoid its taking place. The territory envisaged as abandoned without combat will not in fact be abandoned as aggression will not take place, but it constitutes a very strong deterrent argument which it is important to utilize.

3. The credibility of the use of tactical atomic weapons, as emphasized above, can be measurably increased by research and the development of "cleaner" tactical atomic weapons which would allow us to justify, and thus make less improbable, the use of a relatively increased number of nuclear weapons on the battlefield. These studies would have a deterrent value, so there are reasons to return to them.

V. CONSEQUENCES FOR THE CONCEPT OF FORCES

The operational conception of tactical nuclear weapons in view of the deterrent action that we have just examined requires that a whole series of operational and strategic-tactical pre-conditions have been fulfilled. This body of conditions, at least in tactical and operational spheres, requires a revision in the concept of forces, to obtain the best deterrent dividend from them.

In fact, in their present concept, Western forces, apart from visibly lacking operational agility and use of nuclear weapons, necessarily lead to extremely unstable battle formulae, which are thus quite dangerous. To realize a more stable disposition, and thus a better deterrence, it is absolutely necessary that their volume be increased, necessarily leading to reducing forces from "level 2": and summoning up forces from "level 3." In sum, the deterrent formula to be realized consists of carrying out a more logical distribution between missions of highly technical forces with costly equipment and the more simple, more economical forces.

The mobile screen

The first example of this revision relies on the establishment of a mobile and continuous screen which must cover the whole of the front.

In its current conception, this screen is provided by forces of high maneuvera-bility, thus by limited and expensive forces. In order to establish it, we are led to spread dispersed divisions along fronts ranging from 50 to 100 kilometers. In the theatre of central Europe with its 700 kilometers of front, this requires a commitment of about ten divisions, that is to say half the forces, for a simple security mission. It is true that, in addition, we count upon this screen to be supported by divisions in immediate reserve to take the battle into its initial conventional phase, in which nearly all the powerful means available will be risked.

From the time when it becomes a question of meeting the enemy advance and of slowing it a bit by destruction and harassment, it is a waste to use well-equipped divisions which should be reserved for counter-offensive opera-tions with nuclear weapons. On the contrary, the system of forward safety for the whole of the army can be economically constituted by units of *motorized militia,* provided with the best anti-tank armament and with a very thoroughly studied communications system for interior liaison and for long-distance intelli-gence. An example of what such a motorized militia could be in a formula which perhaps appears revolutionary, but not utopian, is outlined in the Appendix. The existence of such a militia would allow us to keep in reserve all, or almost all, of the powerful units for the battle proper.

The strength of these motorized militia must be such that it effectively covers all of the front and thus depends directly on the width of the front. Naturally, this needed strength can only be realized by a system of *local mobilization* of reservists specially trained for this mission and periodically called up for short periods of maneuvers.

A way to mobilize three yearly contingents of such militia units is presented in the Appendix. The formulae indicated here should be considered solutions intended to stimulate the imagination and not, of course, as model examples. The entire strength of these territorial militia must be sufficient to assure a good density of occupation over the whole of the national territory.

The counter-offensive battle

To lead the counter-offensive battle, whose threat must be deterrent, is a matter of being able to combine the following actions:

1. powerful tactical nuclear weapons with rapid launching potential;

2. air defense missions accomplishing an appropriate interception at battle-field level (surface-air missiles and interceptor fighters);

3. air support missions for information and fire;

4. large mechanized elements whose number should be proportional to equivalent enemy forces, ready in dispersed units, to offensively exploit possible atomic firing;

5. eventually certain large airmobile units constituting a strategic reserve or acting in depth against the enemy force if the air situation permits.

All these means, largely based in depth under the protection of the ground defense forces, constitute the element of maneuver which is needed by the military command as a threat or for acting according to need.

Perspectives for evolution

In the first analysis, it seems that each of the categories of forces enumerated above can be redefined in a more precise way in order to take into account the evolution to be foreseen in armaments and with forces for possible combat.

Mechanized forces would be reviewed in order to adapt them in relation to development of teleguided antitank weapons. The evolution forecast is the replacement of the heavily armored tank with a high-caliber cannon by a much lighter, less-armored tank, armed with anti-personnel and anti-tank (probably radio-guided) means of offensive firing and protected by teleguided anti-tank weapons supported by saturation artillery fire and accompanied by armored infantry. The armor protection for all these units should be able to withstand fire from light arms, fragmentation bombs and effects of heat and fallout from nuclear explosions.

The airmobile forces would be reorganized according to their adaptability to helicopters and to their land mobility (addition of bicycles, vehicles and light tanks).

Forces delivering nuclear weapons are of two different categories: those in direct support, supplying the organic fire to divisions (range of 50 to 100 kilometers) and *general support forces* of a minimum range of 200 kilometers and a maximum of 500.

Tactical air forces seem to evolve towards the development of ground-to-air missiles and ground-to-ground missiles. Correlatively, piloted combat planes, which are of necessity short take-off or vertical take-off capability (STOL or VTOL), would be more and more reduced. For transportation, the helicopter and the short take-off plane will become more and more indispensable.

Militia forces, composed of light divisions with all types of arms—portable weapons, vehicles, mortar artillery—must include some infantry divisions for surface defense, cavalry divisions for the mobile system, and mountain divisions.

VI. CONCLUSIONS

I am ending considerations here. With a little imagination and a lot of optimism, I have sought to define the optimum conditions to be fulfilled for a *totally deterrent character* at the tactical nuclear level, now an absolute necessity in politically sensitive areas because of the fundamental instability of conventional warfare which has become, because of this, eminently dangerous.

I will not defend here each of the partial solutions which I have proposed because I do not claim to present complete and sure solutions, but wish only to emphasize the necessity and the possibility of carrying out a fundamental revision in our concept relative to battle, as well as in the general articulation of forces which appears logical in terms of present perspectives. It is certain that the atomic weapon, the present discontinuity and dispersion of troops impose important modifications in the structure and eventual use of forces.

Carrying out this revision in terms of the present defense system of NATO, Sokolowski and his collaborators have arrived at building a determinedly offensive doctrine which effectively risks baffling the provisions of the defense.

In this abstract war which is carried on "in time of peace," by armed forces which envisage the possibility of having to fight some day, it is important, on our part, to carry out a revision capable of baffling the enemy offensive plan and thus to deter it. This deterrence is based in the conception of a *much more stable defensive strategy*, thus one which is much more in depth and powerful, as well as less discontinuous. In particular, the necessity for the maneuvering forces to be able to be totally devoted to the eventual battle, thus operating in an atmosphere of security provided by the militia, seems to be one of the least contestable conclusions. It is possible, and even probable, that this method of reinforcing the conventional forces of "level 2" by the militia of "level 3" may allow for the realization of a *deterrence of conventional war, capable of considerably raising the threshold of nuclear weapons* and, through this, adoption of a system of deterrence which is both more effective and less dangerous and giving the armed forces, and thus its commanding officers, a coherent doctrine which may give them confidence—which is not the case at present.[1] In addition, by doing this, we are preparing ourselves more efficiently for the not improbable hypothesis of a revolutionary war.

In any case, while waiting to be able to establish a military system such as the one proposed here, it is essential to restore the credibility of the generalized and early use of tactical atomic weapons, by an appropriate, clearly-displayed strategy. This strategy must be founded on the unknown psychological effect of nuclear explosions. *It is only in this way that we will be able to maintain an effective deterrent value at the tactical nuclear level.*

---

[1] See the manifesto of the 30 German Captains.

Chapter V

REFLECTIONS ON THE NAVY

It is not without hesitation that I embark on this chapter on the Navy because I must admit that my technical and tactical competence in the area is quite weak. However, I do not think I can treat present over-all military problems without including the Navy. Thus I will do it by attempting to limit myself to considerations drawn from the historical evolution and total strategy of conflicts, avoiding as much as possible consideration of internal problems—as I did in other chapters—in which technical details play such an important part. It will, in a sense, be a study from the outside, and if I should make too gross errors, I hope the experts will not be too critical of me.

I. THE EVOLUTION OF THE NAVY

Since earliest days, the Navy has had as its object the domination of maritime spaces in order to prohibit their use by the adversary. This domination, founded on the existence of fleets and naval bases, was practiced through victorious naval battles aiming at *physical destruction* of enemy ships. Indeed, in contradiction to what happens on land, the cohesion of the crew was assured by the ships they served. A sailor cannot save himself except through his ship. It is very rare throughout history that a fleet becomes disorganized in the way armies disintegrate. When a fleet had bad morale, this was translated into a propensity for avoiding combat, but the fleet remained alive as long as the ships were not sunk. From another point of view, naval battle has almost always been very rapidly and very completely decisive—a little like ancient land battles. This important characteristic has obliged the various navies to develop highly appropriate tactical procedures and to follow naval strategies which allow for refusing battle (the sea is wide) except in favorable conditions.

Naval combat, like land combat, constantly evolved as weapons changed and it has led to forms of battle which are less and less alike. In the beginning, battles were carried out by ramming (Salamis) or by capturing ships by boarding. It was, in a word, Infantry—hand to hand combat, very similar to siege warfare of the time. With the appearance of artillery, naval battles were carried on at cannonball distance in order to cripple enemy ships which were then boarded and taken. When artillery became more powerful, ships were sunk by artillery duels at a distance, in spite of the gradual development of armor-plating. With this appearance of artillery, firepower (and the maneuverability of sail boats, then steamships) led to the decisive superiority of the stronger. Tactics, notably those of evasion, played a role, but the central element of the battle was of a technical nature, much earlier so than in land armies.

This race to power led to the construction of bigger and bigger warships with heavier and heavier arms and, ultimately, to the "dreadnought" which called itself an absolute weapon for, according to its name, it feared nothing, because of its weaponry and armor-plating. Following this, came a new tendency which is not without analogy with what we have called levels 2 and 3 in land armies. The large armored ship could become a prey for smaller and more rapid ships which possessed a very powerful weapon, the torpedo.[1] First came the torpedo boats, then the submarines. At this point new classes of light boats or anti-torpedo boats and anti-submarines were born. Like the land armies, the Navy then became a complex ensemble of elements with different characteristics which had to be combined with tactical methods. Simultaneously, a new technique, mining, tended to set up permanent maritime obstacles. At the time of the First World War, naval warfare had become so complicated that fleets hesitated to engage in pitched battle. The potential weight of naval armaments determined the action zones of various fleets which no longer clashed except in a

---

[1] Note motor torpedo boats and frogmen.

sort of naval guerilla action based on the use of small boats and submarines. The efforts of the navies, which we will later discuss again, directed themselves towards attack and defense of the sea lanes.

At the time of the Second World War, the appearance of the air forces (based on land or on ships) and aircraft carriers revolutionized naval tactics and strategy. The big naval battles in the Pacific and the liquidation of the German pocket cruisers in the Atlantic were the work of the air forces. Air superiority at sea, as well as on land, became the decisive element. It was no longer the weight of "fleets in being" which determined the action zone of fleets, but the radius of action of air bases and aircraft carriers. On board, artillery lost a good part of its importance.

But technical evolution does not stop. In the period following the war, progress and development in long-distance sea weapons, as well as in anti-air, sea-to-air weapons modified the preceding data. Naval combat with very powerful weapons no longer necessitated ships with great tonnage; ships can operate at very great distances supplied by homing weapons and aided by reconnaissance which, on the flat surface of the sea, cannot miss the target ship. The airplane tends to lose its supremacy unless operating with the aid of air-to-sea weapons shot into areas beyond the reach of the aerial defenses of ships. A whole tactical revolution is evolving, and doubtless is still barely unleashed.

At the same time, other factors appear: nuclear propulsion which confers on fleets a speed and radius of action once unthought of; the development of submarines; and especially the possible use of tactical and strategic atomic weaponry. All of these simultaneous innovations create problems which are very difficult to decipher since it is not necessarily a question of naval battle and since future innovations must keep in mind the role expected of Navies, in wartime and in peace.

II. EVOLUTION OF THE ROLE OF THE SEA IN CONFLICT

The sea has played very different roles throughout the course of history: sometimes it is a question of transporting invasion forces, sometimes of opening commercial routes, sometimes of eliminating the enemy's commercial routes. Sometimes the sea has constituted the decisive operational theater, sometimes it has played only an auxiliary role. Naturally, all of these variations have been produced by the general and geo-strategic conditions of conflict, which today we should call "total strategy", in which the economic and commercial roles of the sea are included. In continental conflicts (the Franco-Prussian War of 1870, the Italian War of 1854), the sea has not played an important role. However, when the continent was confronted by a sea power (wars of the French Empire, the First and Second World Wars) it could be maintained that the mastery of the sea gave a decisive superiority to the sea powers over the continental powers. This is the well known theory of Mahan, justified by the growing economic importance of the sea, and thus of the blockade, and by the strategic mobility of land forces made possible by the sea. Moreover, since they could not be attacked across the sea, maritime powers could carry on "protracted wars" and practice against their continental adversary a strategy of peripheral threats. This theory has been fully confirmed by the Second World War in which the initial naval superiority of Japan gave the whole of Southeast Asia to her, while later naval defeat reduced her to capitulation. In Europe, the continental victory of Germany—checked, it is true, in Russia—was in large part annulled by the peripheral Allied action in North Africa, Italy, and in France. The Navy, in its aero-naval form of the era, then played an essential role which was at the same time logistic, operational and strategic.

After the war, within the NATO framework, the eventual role of the sea gave rise to important debates stemming from the appearance of nuclear arms. Two essential problems were brought out:

Did atomic arms permit the survival of surface fleets?

Would nuclear warfare, necessarily short in any case, maintain the major logistic role that the Navy played during the Second World War?

These two problems, as is usually the case during periods of rapid evolution, were badly stated, since the character of future warfare itself remained very poorly defined. NATO believed at first in the inevitability of a nuclear "paroxysm" war with the generalized use of nuclear arms. In this hypothesis, not only did surface fleets have precarious survival, but even the existence of ports became problematic—as did, moreover, the existence of populations. As this "spasm" war appeared less and less possible, and as ideas concentrated on the concept of deterrence, new possibilities appeared.

On the one hand, *the sea became the privileged domain of deterrence* through the appearance of missile-carrying nuclear-powered submarines, practically undetectable because of their impenetrability by electronic devices in the sea environment.

On the other hand, the phenomenon of deterrence carried with it the evolution of war towards *limited forms,* indeed conventional forms, in which surface fleets, particularly aircraft carriers and amphibious crafts, could play a major role.

The Navy, therefore, discovered a considerable importance under new or renewed forms. Its intervention in the Cuban crisis, its action in Vietnam, its presence in the Mediterranean during the Middle East crisis showed that the Navy holds a political and strategic interest of the first order under its conceptual form. The development of missile-carrying nuclear submarines made it the back bone of strategic deterrence. Moreover, basing itself on these observations, the Soviets began to develop a considerable naval force almost equal to that of the Americans and notably superior in the submarine sphere.

It, therefore, seems today that the naval problem has become relatively clear. As in the ground-air domain, we have come to distinguish between the levels of strategic nuclear deterrence, conventional warfare and tactical nuclear deterrence; in the naval sphere, we have been led to the same categorizations. However, the consequences are different at each level. A new concept of fleets has become necessary.

III. VARIOUS CATEGORIES OF NAVAL FORCES

At the level of *strategic nuclear deterrence,* it very rapidly became apparent that the existence of missile-carrying submarines carries with it the need to foresee a new kind of submarine and anti-submarine warfare, requiring the combination of very diverse surface equipment, submarine and aerial equipment. Considering the key importance of strategic deterrence, it is evident that the constitution of this auxiliary and complementary fleet (to nuclear submarines) possesses an absolute priority. It remains to be seen which are the most effective materials and tactics, a problem which is doubtless only in the process of solution. Naturally, the importance of the projected means depends on the number of submarines to be protected. The operation would be more costly in a national framework than in an alliance.

At *the level of conventional warfare* of a limited character, traditional ships adapted to the new sea-to-air weapons (without nuclear warheads) maintain a considerable political and strategic interest. They constitute, along with landed ground troops, an *intervention force* whose role and importance depend on the interests to be defended in the politics pursued and the envisioned strategies. Taking into account their high price, their volume is necessarily reduced, just as in the land forces of "level 2". Its minimum volume is that of a national force having all of the elements necessary for an intervention of sufficient political value. This very vague definition necessarily includes an aircraft carrier and a helicopter carrier, as well as protective and support naval forces whose weaponry, now doubtless on the basis of missiles, permits the use of ships of lesser tonnage.

At *the level of tactical nuclear deterrence,* the Navy poses a special problem. It is not a question of dissuading a conventional aggression aiming at the *fait accompli,* as it is on land, a phenomenon due to the inherent instability of conventional ground warfare. On the sea, so far as we can clearly see in this sphere, it is a question of dissuading an adversary from seeking a naval decision by the surprise use of weapons with nuclear heads in a war which would have a limited character. It is therefore indispensable to have ships armed with nuclear warheads and confer on these ships a certain protection against the nuclear fallout especially important on the sea, so as to be able to respond. It would therefore be a matter of simple adaptation of conventional forces, as it is done on land (protection, dispersion, etc . . .). All the same, Navy people often think that if limited nuclear warfare is hardly probable on land, it is because deterrence works, and because civilized populations would be involved. It remains less improbable on the sea since it would only be a question of a duel between purely military forces and taking place in the neutral territory of the high seas. I do not believe very much in this possibility because of various inhibitions which weigh against the use of nuclear arms, but it may be said that it is in the naval sphere that such a use is the least improbable.

However, on the sea there exists another level, the one of *intercontinental logistics*. It has played an enormous role in the course of the two world wars, and the development of a considerable submarine fleet by the Soviets permits us to conceive of the possibility of *conventional blockade warfare*. This prospect, quite difficult to imagine politically, is militarily realizable. It would become part of an implacable submarine warfare directed against missile-carrying nuclear submarines and would make the sea the essential operational theater. This, perhaps, is what the rapid growth of the Soviet war fleet announces, which perhaps has conceived of the same offensive project undertaken by the Soviet Army, and envisages one day being able to conduct a decisive naval war. This could even include a landing in the United States by repeating in the polar regions from islands and ice fields the same strategy set up by the Americans in the Pacific. The prodigious growth of the Soviet merchant fleet would render it possible.

IV. CONCLUSIONS

Whatever the dreams which have inspired the authors of Soviet programs—dreams which are visibly either very late or very early with regard to the policies presently practiced by the Kremlin—we cannot deny the importance of the evolution which has taken place in these last years. Nor can we underestimate the crucial character of maritime spaces, especially their depths, because of the growing role of submarines, but also with respect to the surface area which allow parties to carry their flag into faraway seas with a sort of political propaganda in mind. This has not lost its value judging by the Soviet infiltration in the Red Sea and the Indian Ocean.

A fleet, much more than an army, is a slowly forged tool. After British naval supremacy, we witnessed a fairly long period of American naval supremacy. This risks giving away to Soviet quasi-supremacy if the Americans are not alert. This is a very important strategic event. Does it correspond to a logical plan or is it a late result of Khrushchev's discomfort in Cuba? We cannot say. On the other hand, the Soviet policy of rapprochement with the United States and its growing opposition to China does not seem to justify such an effort, unless it is to obtain a balance with the Americans in all spheres and of facilitating a sort of sharing of the world through it. In any case, the Soviet naval tool has become considerable and cannot miss having an important political and strategic influence.

What we should clearly see is that the evolution of the phenomenon of strategic nuclear deterrence opens up major possibilities for the Navy in the sphere of deterrence while it gives conventional fleets an active role in conventional warfare as well as in world political strategy.

If we place ourselves in the perspective which I outlined in the chapter on the level of strategic nuclear deterrence—the great probable conflict in the 21st Century for the domination of world organizations whose development is in the order of things—it must be remembered that naval forces will have an important role to play, since it will be essentially a world conflict.

This vision of the future, which unfortunately is not improbable, cannot but justify a national effort in the maritime sphere and also a collective effort within the framework of Europe, as soon as the necessary political pre-conditions have been set.

Chapter VI

GENERAL CONCLUSIONS

The immediately preceding discussion of the Navy, through its synthetic character, leads us into general conclusions on the problems of the military.

I. OVERALL DIAGNOSIS

To attempt an overall diagnosis requires recognition of the delicate and subtle character of military problems. Remedies must be adapted to the extreme complexity of situations created by the phenomenon of the existence and use of military forces both in action and as a deterrent.

This phenomenon, long misunderstood or unclear, is readily clarified if each level of the use of force is examined separately.

1. On the level of total nuclear war ("spasm" nuclear war), it is evident that such warfare becomes *impossible as soon as it is bilateral.* The reciprocal destruction that results is senseless for both adversaries. On the other hand,

nuclear warfare would be absolutely decisive if only one of the adversaries possessed nuclear arms. In this case the threat of the use of the arms alone would constitute an irresistible blackmail. It follows that to avoid this, it has become necessary to neutralize strategic nuclear arms by a reciprocal threat. This has the effect of realizing strategic nuclear deterrence.

This *deterrence* which has for a time been believed capable of affecting other levels of the use of force, and to protect allies not provided with nuclear arms tends to see its role restricted to the mutually menacing nuclear powers. Strategic nuclear deterrence has become almost an absolute necessity for nations gravely menaced by their political or geo-strategic situation[1] which cannot be replaced by any exterior guarantees as long as a true system of world security, supplied with adequate armaments, is not achieved in the foreseeable future. While awaiting such a system, an increase in the number of nuclear powers is probable.

2. On the level of conventional warfare (without nuclear weapons) it has become evident that this form of war remains *possible,* but that it has come in our day to take on a new and specific role. It is strictly limited in order to avoid destruction out of proportion with the political objectives of the conflict, to avoid raising the opposition of world opinion, and to avoid the risk of escalating the conflict, notably by its extension to the nuclear powers. Conventional war has therefore remained a means of international action, but its limitation at least prevents it from attaining overly-ambitious political results.

Nevertheless, it happens that the actual operational conditions (greatly reduced volume of highly mobile forces) confer very rapid military decisions following confrontations of conventional forces. Conventional warfare thus conducted is extremely unstable; it can be viewed as a very tempting means of action to resolve political problems perceived to be important by a *fait accompli.* It is therefore becoming necessary to find military formulae capable of stabilizing the level of conventional war by well-adapted means of deterrence.

3. Deterrence on the level of conventional warfare appears to be capable of realization by three categories of procedure:

a. The most simple means would seem to be possession of an assured and *overwhelming aerial superiority,* even in case of surprise. This policy leads to an onerous course of aerial armaments and is without effect against an opponent deploying an equally powerful air force.

---

[1] Happily, there also exists *"moral deterrence."*

b. A second policy, with considerable operational yield (as has been seen in Vietnam) is to threaten invading conventional forces with the use of a popular guerilla war. This policy presupposes the existence of a popular will, visibly prepared to withstand the sacrifices entailed by this form of warfare, as well as of a terrain whose ruggedness and size favors the guerilla. It can be applied to the developed States of Western Europe only very poorly.

c. A third policy consists of menacing invading conventional forces with the use of *tactical atomic weapons.* This threat is highly dissuasive if the adversary does not possess nuclear weapons. If it does possess them, it is dissuasive in that a *bilateral* tactical nuclear battle is almost unforeseeable and probably impractical. The threat of using tactical atomic weapons is therefore both a deterrent to conventional aggression and to the enemy's use of tactical atomic weapons. It is, therefore, *essentially a level of deterrence.* This characteristic risks some proliferation of tactical atomic weapons in politically sensitive regions where recourse to guerilla war is difficult. Naturally, this threat is credible only to the extent that tactical and operational procedures have been adapted towards it.

As has been seen, the military means must respond simultaneously to these diverse imperatives, on the land, on the sea, in the air and, indeed, in space.

Thus, what characterizes the modern era from the military point of view is *the coexistence of deterrence and action.* Deterrence is effected by means specific to each given level of the use of force. Military action is normally effected in the conventional style in the framework defined by the more complex factors of total strategy. The central element of deterrence (there are others) is the nuclear weapon, both strategic and tactical, of which the effect has been multiplied by its exploitation by the "mass media". The action of military forces benefits equally from the psychological influence of the mass media.

II. SOLUTION OF MILITARY PROBLEMS

These complex military problems cannot be logically resolved except by taking into consideration the individual possibilities of the various technical levels determined by armaments and materials.

1. What we have called *"level 0",* which calls for the most advanced scientific techniques, is virtually reserved for the superpowers. Their constant progress is such that the superpowers are searching—futilely, probably—to freeze their development. It is possible that, in the relatively near future, "level 0" will be accessible only to a power enjoying considerable means of action, which would mean in the end a truly world power or an international authority. This almost

fatal tendency towards the globalization of "level 0" opens particularly serious perspectives and poses difficult problems from here on.

2. What we call *"level 1"*, in other words, that of strategic and tactical nuclear weapons, reveals itself to be accessible to middle nations and probably, in the future, to small nations, despite the already elaborate techniques, because these techniques will be progressively at the disposal of all States. From this results a perspective of *proliferation* which presents two contradictory aspects. Within certain limits, proliferation tends to extend the zone of action of deterrence—therefore military peace. Beyond these limits, it augments the possibility of irresponsible use of nuclear weapons (notably by nuclear guerillas) which would create a characteristically unbearable instability. It can almost be imagined that the necessary outcome of this tendency will be the institution of an international authority possessing the necessary means of deterrence. One finds here the same subjects for serious consideration: the tendency towards globalization already encountered in "level 0".

Let us note, moreover, that it is possible that evolution will one day confer an absolute domination by "level 0" over "level 1".

3. What we have called *"level 2"*, in other words, the level of highly technical conventional armaments (planes, teleguided anti-aircraft and anti-tank missiles, armored vehicles, surface and submarine warships, radar, radio telecommunications, etc.) is evidently accessible to middle and small nations, but their cost is so high that the strength of these forces is far from sufficient to play a decisive military role. From this results a tendency among the small and middle powers to obtain the necessary armaments from a foreign protector (Egypt and Israel) or to combine the forces of several nations in the framework of an alliance (case of NATO). These tendencies will develop only with waning sophistication of the materials of "level 2." It is certain that all kinds of imperatives of mass industrial production are more and more opposed to the small artisanal production by national industries. Zones of common market of armaments, defined as a function of political factors, are at this moment desirable and probable.

4. What we have called *"level 3"* is that of simple, inexpensive and unsophisticated materials, constituting an *essentially national level.* Suitably used, it plays an indispensable role in the military and moral survival of nations in a world becoming more and more globalized.

In its extreme form, it can lead to forms of popular war, providing that the political and psychological environment justifies it. However, we have proposed a formula in Chapter IV, combining "level 2" and "level 3." This appears to be the most logical solution under the present estimates of nuclear threat and the possibilities of conventional and revolutionary war. I have been persuaded that the system of *national militia* complemented by limited forces of "level 2," that I recommended several years ago, will not fail to know a major development in Europe as it has on other continents. With a greatly reduced standing military force, this would be a return to a concept of efficiently protecting the instinct of defending the fatherland in association with the effective and accessible means of the population defending its soil. This system, which already exists in very diverse forms in Sweden, Switzerland and Yugoslavia, is beginning to be introduced in Germany and is recommended by several American theoreticians.

There remains, we will see, the need to resolve in polished form the great dilemma confronting armies by the problem of transition from peace into war.

III. THE ESSENTIAL MILITARY DILEMMA

In effect, the most difficult military problem to resolve is that of establishing a security system, as inexpensive as possible in time of peace, capable of transforming itself very rapidly into a powerful force in case of the danger of aggression.

This contradictory necessity impels military forces to be capable of continually adapting to political fluctuations—as well as to technical progress. While politics is essentially variable, military forces demonstrate great inertia because of their material and the slow realization of programs. Two extreme solutions are therefore conceivable: to be ready at all times for an important conflict (the NATO solution) accepting a permanent effort which constitutes a definite waste during periods of calm; or to wait until the moment of danger before developing armaments (the American system in 1917 and 1941) which presupposes that distance and oceans act as protection. The German solution which consists of rearming in view of a war that is to be launched at a pre-determined date is applicable only to nations maintaining aggressive designs.

The defensive solution consists essentially of creating military institutions of a minimum strength and cost during periods of full peace and structured so that they lend themselves to successive reinforcement in response to the political situation without reorganization. This is the principle of the *"inflatable army,"* always adaptable to the evaluation of the risk of war. This solution can include two kinds of inflation: a slow and progressive style—therefore evolutionary—launching the production of armaments and increasing the duration of active military service, etc., and a quasi-instantaneous style through mechanisms of mobilization and requisition. This formula was that of armies at the turn of the century. The belief in the inescapability of a spasm nuclear war instantly developing has brought NATO to challenge in practice the principle of mobilization. Now that it is clear that the risk of conventional warfare remains, but that this risk will not suddenly appear without being announced by a given political situation, *it has become indispensable to return to mobilization.* From this point of view, the system of national militia presents extensive possibilities because too costly "level 2" forces will neither "inflate" extensively nor, above all, quickly. "Level 3", through its inexpensive armaments and through its extended recourse to requisition, alone presents itself as greatly and rapidly expandable.

From now on, the solution to the military dilemma consists of practicing a very careful permanent strategy of adapting the importance of military forces to the evolution of the political solution and the dangers that are born from it—a condition in which the minimum formula is calculated exactly to be the most inexpensive possible and in which the means to permit changes of volume without reorganization are preconceived.

I am convinced that this is the formula of the future in the period that we are approaching.

IV. THE FUTURE OF THE ARMED FORCES

Having come to the end of our inquiry into military problems, it is legitimate to ask ourselves what the future of the armed forces is. This question is not without purpose at a moment when there exists a sort of fashion—very recent and, moreover, very localized—that proclaims the end of wars, considered to be scandalous relics, and the purposelessness and harmfulness of military armaments. In addition, the phenomenon of nuclear deterrence has founded great hopes for the suppression of war; deterrence no more suppresses war than antibiotics suppress disease since disease continues to play its demographic role by other means. The attitude of a genius, for example, of the level of Einstein— who nevertheless recommended atomic weapons—is characteristic in this instance of the almost irresponsible lack of reality with which problems relating to national defense are considered in certain circles of opinion.

To respond to this question with objectivity, it is necessary to recognize that the future of armed forces essentially depends upon the evolution of international politics during the coming century: whether it will or will not settle the existing tensions and if it will succeed or not in establishing an effective system of international arbitration. From this, several possible futures result, although of unequal probability.

1. If we are led to imagine that the present conjecture will not be greatly modified in its nature, one may predict the permanence of the modern tendencies that we have recognized. These are characterized by the maintenance of national realities at several stages, from the small nations through the large, by the essentially technical tendency to globalize more and more important and

numerous problems, as well as by the inevitability of alliances between nations when dangerous international tensions appear. This reasonably probable perspective is that which I call *the classic vision of the international future.*

Under this hypothesis, it is evident that the armed forces will retain their present role, both as deterrents and as active forces, in the service of politics. Their national and occasionally inter-allied mission will stay intact. Nevertheless, the probable development of several organizations with global jurisdictions will introduce a new dimension into various military problems, probably in the sense of the limitation of conflicts.

2. If it is believed, on the other hand, that humanity is effectively heading towards a sincere renunciation of violence—which presupposes a serious change in human nature—it is possible to admit the possibility of the realization of an effective system of international arbitration. This is an already ancient hope which has had a role at the turn of the century with the creation of the Hague tribunal, later with the creation of the League of Nations and finally with the creation of the United Nations and its Security Council. It cannot be said, at present, that these attempts have really demonstrated effectiveness. They often—or, at least, sometimes—play a useful role, but their failure to recognize the organic nature of reality within international dynamics has completely disarmed them in the face of the major tempests since the Second World War. Decolonization and the Middle Eastern crisis are examples. It is certain that a more realistic vision would have to lead to the creation of a truly international force, of which the blue helmets are a mere caricature. Moreover, the existence of a real international force poses the crucial problem of the creation of a real international authority, a creation which appears to be virtually unattainable at the present time.

Whatever it is, this perspective—which I will term *the optimistic vision of the international future* (to avoid saying utopian)—does not involve the elimination of the armed forces, but their internationalization, at least on level 0, 1, and perhaps 2. Only level 3 would remain strictly national.

3. Finally, it is possible to imagine, as we have seen repeatedly in this study, that the technical tendency of globalization involves a great world conflict to decide which of the great modern civilizations will have the privilege of making its mark on the inevitably developing world institutions. With the view of history evolving only in a one-way direction (the past displaying successive pulsations) this would be "the ultimate struggle" before the unification of the planet. Moreover, as I demonstrated in *L'Enjeu du Désordre,*[1] it is to be thought that

---

[1] *The Stakes of Disorder,* Grasset, Paris, 1969.

adaptation to the rapid evolution of our societies may lead to violent revolution-ary-style crises and, similarly, to international conflicts akin to the Spanish Civil War. These perspectives, that I will call *the pessimistic vision of the international future,* are far from being improbable, without much assurance that this will be "the ultimate conflict." This is a hypothesis that must be considered. It would give considerable importance to the armed forces.

In conclusion, let us say that these three classic, optimistic and pessimistic visions constitute as many possibilities of which it is impossible to completely eliminate any of them. These three futures coexist for us and we must be prepared to adapt ourselves to them in time, according to the possibilities of their transforming themselves into probabilities. This should be the major preoccupation of politicians and strategists.

However, while waiting for these very different futures to define themselves, it appears indispensable to me to work with the classic solution. This is to forecast, at this time, the maintenance of national realities, the progressive and measured tendency towards the globalization of a certain number of technical problems of world importance and the inevitability of alliances when the political situation requires them.

Within this perspective, *the role and importance of military forces cannot decrease.* Western public opinion must recognize this reality. Those who con-tinue to be interested in military careers should be reassured. Their future remains similar to that of their predecessors. History evolves, but the phenomena to which it gives birth, although different in form, remain strangely the same in essence.

Annex

A DETAILED EXAMPLE
OF THE ORGANIZATION
OF TERRITORIAL MILITIA*

The following note on the organization of territorial units constitutes a good example of a theoretical solution which is rather tempting in my opinion, because it allows for the establishment of a mobile screen and of a surface defense of quite some efficiency with a budgetary load in peace-time of 150,000 men, while it can call on, with three contingents of draftees recalled yearly, a force of six mobile defense divisions and 54 ground defense divisions: a total of 60 divisions. In addition, it would lead, for the great majority of the draftees, to reducing the length of service to 4 months, followed by two or three recalls of three weeks during the summer. In this solution, the some 70,000 draftees necessary for the main battle, for the infrastructure and for operating training centers of the territorial units would be supplied by volunteers of one year

---

*Hereinafter referred to as the OTD (Organized Territorial Defense).

receiving special extra benefits: bonuses, learning a military specialty, not being periodically called up except during war time.

It is very evident that other solutions are imaginable. But this one, justified by sufficient details, shows that very different formulae exist from those in effect today. The one proposed here also has the advantage of allowing a very progressive enlargement of OTD forces, without any reorganization.

I wish that this example could stimulate the imagination of the planners and that if not adopted as is (which would astonish me) it would lead to interesting accomplishments in this area which I deem vital, and which does not seem to me to be sufficiently considered at present.

May they see in this solution a modern equivalent of the *Rêveries* which Marshal de Saxe presented as the fruit of his experience and of his reflections.

ORGANIZATION OF OTD UNITS

Overall Considerations

The study made on the general problem of battle has emphasized the necessity of filling two categories of indispensable military needs in order to frame and prolong the action of forces in combat elements; needs which can only be satisfied by OTD units.

1. Establishment on any threatened frontier, of a mobile screen capable of blocking and harassing enemy invasion forces.

2. Establishment on all national territory, of a surface defense combining military area responsibility by units guarding a given portion of the land with the possible use of attacking combat units.

It is, on the other hand, evident that these needs, calculated accurately, must be able to be filled effectively by calling up a small number of yearly "classes" of draftees (in principle not more than three). These two categories of imperatives allow for the definition of a coherent military system which will be set forth in the appendices which follow.

Finally, it appeared during the course of the study that the conditions decided on for establishing a mobile screen corresponded rather well (with some modifications) to the needs of ground defense units. This last consideration justifies a certain unity of structure which also considerably simplifies the study of the problem.

Military System of OTD Units

A complete ground or surface defense covered by a mobile screen demands on the order of 60 Divisions of 14,000 men of the type which will be defined later. This would make 840,000 men, which represents roughly three yearly "classes" of 300,000 draftees. The simultaneous calling of three classes represents an important political measure except in the case of immediate danger. So it is necessary to proportion out the call-ups by class and even by half class. This necessity demands that the OTD units be constituted in a homogeneous manner by men of the same half class. The problem comes back then to making with each half class (150,000 men) ten OTD Divisions, one per region, and to further organizing in each region, the calling up and equipping of the five half classes held in reserve. Each region would thus produce six OTD Divisions, two per year.

The length of active duty in the OTD units would be four months, followed each year by summer periods of three weeks for three years. The total length of service would thus be six months. The budgetary strength would be 150,000 men. Career cadres of the OTD forces would be on the order of 20,000 officers and men. Appendix I, which follows, sets forth the possible organization and training schedule of this military service.

This conception can be realized in the framework of a land army of about 300,000 men, assuming 190,000 career officers and soldiers (we have only 120,000) or of having 70,000 short-term volunteers doing two years (at 35,000 volunteers per year); or otherwise 70,000 draftees doing one year with certain benefits. The OTD contingents would then be reduced to 110,000 men per half contingent (See Table 1).

Table 1

Classification	Total	Long-term career soldiers	Draftees 1 year	Draftees 6 months
Combat troops	100,000	80,000	20,000	
Infrastructure	50,000	20,000	30,000	
OTD units.	150,000	20,000	20,000	110,000
	300,000	120,000	70,000	110,000

Conception and Structure of OTD Units

OTD units are conceived in direct terms of their mission. Their structure, as rational as possible, is based on the following principles:

1. Integral motorization with civil vehicles. The basis of organization is the civil car carrying five men.

2. Light and inexpensive armament.

3. Standard structure with variation in weapons and equipment in order to adapt to the three essential missions:
   a) mobile screen;
   b) surface defense on average terrain;
   c) surface defense in mountains.
   Organic distinction between (i) *commando units* for surface defense and harassment, and (ii) *attack units* for actions of force, possibly in strength.

4. Economical structures. Essentially regional logistics founded on territorial resources; less rigid chains of command, important from the communications point of view, by placing the greatest number of subordinate units under the same commander, yet giving him deputies to lead temporary groups.

The application of these principles leads to a definition of the detailed structure of the divisions of the "mobile screen" or mobile defense, and of the surface defense divisions. These are summarized in Appendices II and III below.

Appendix 1

ORGANIZATION OF OTD UNIT INSTRUCTION

The OTD units, almost completely composed of men from the same half-contingent, receive accelerated training by Battalion or Squadron Group.

First month:
75% recruits and 25% cadres and veterans; assignment and basic training.

Second month:
Platoon of NCO specialist students; beginning of specialized training.

Third month:
Group school; nomination of cadres from the contingent.

Fourth month:
Unit training (Section and Platoon); end active duty; return to reserve status.

First recall:
3 weeks the following summer;[1] Company maneuvers in camp.

Second recall:
3 weeks the following summer; Company and Battalion maneuvers.

Third recall:
3 weeks the following summer if necessary **materiel** is available; Large unit (Regiment or Division) maneuvers.

* * *

Training is conducted by the nucleus of a professional cadre and veterans (short-term volunteers or draftees serving one year) who assume unit logistics functions during the first three months. This nucleus is on the order of 25 per cent of the total strength.

The fourth month, the nucleus remains on the spot but in double command in order to supervise the take-over by non-commissioned officers and specialists of the half-contingent.

At the time of the recalls, only a few key functions are filled by the professional staff:

Commanding Officer ....
Company/Squadron Commander
Chief Accountant .... } who were with the unit the fourth month
Chief, Motor Pool .... of active service
Chief, Signal Center, etc. .....

---

[1] If two issues of materiel are not available, either three recalls of two weeks, or two recalls of three weeks can be made.

All other jobs and all platoon commanders are filled by draftees from the half contingent.

*   *   *

Training of reserve officers (who are only officer candidates during their active service) is done in *three months.* They are instructed in a given specialty (Platoon commander, Motor officer, Signal officer, etc.).

*   *   *

OTD units are formed of men from the same military region, complemented if need be, by men from the Paris area. In principle, recruitment is as regional as possible.

Battalion or Squadron Group training centers follow a schedule such as that diagrammed below.

Leaves, organizing Tng Ctr —			
Induction —	January	—	
	February	—	
Instruction of a half contingent —	March	—	
Unit training —	April	—	
	May	—	In camp:
Return to reserve status —		—	Call-up of a half-contingent
Leaves for cadres	June	—	Call-up of a half-contingent
except for 1 % participating in	July	—	Call-up of a half-contingent
the recalls —		—	Call-up of a half contingent
	August	—	Break camp and return to garrison
Induction —			
	September	—	
Instruction of a half-contingent —	October	—	
Unit training —	November	—	
Return to reserve status —	December	—	

A single issue of equipment therefore permits instruction and call-ups of four half-contingents, or two call-ups after active service. If three calls are desired, two issues would be needed or limit the call-up to 15 days.

APPENDIX II

OTD MOBILE DEFENSE DIVISION

Mobile Commando Platoon

The organization rests on the definition of a platoon able to operate on a large front. Its three commando sections supply three patrols of two squads, each operating at one-kilometer intervals, and covers a front of four kilometers. The action of these patrols is backed up by a command and support detachment, employing a section armed with 81-mm mortars on small trucks, capable of engaging personnel throughout the whole zone of action, and also a motorized anti-tank squad using guided missiles for harassing enemy armored spearheads. There are 47 men and 10 vehicles in the platoon.

Field disposition of the platoon is diagrammed in Figure 1.

COMMANDO SECTION (10 men, 2 vehicles)
   Automatic weapons squad (5 men, 1 vehicle)
      4 men, 1 driver
      1 light car, 1 machine gun, 1 grenade launcher

   Rifle squad (5 men, 1 vehicle)
      1 NCO, 3 men, 1 driver
      1 light car, 1 machine gun, 1 rocket launcher

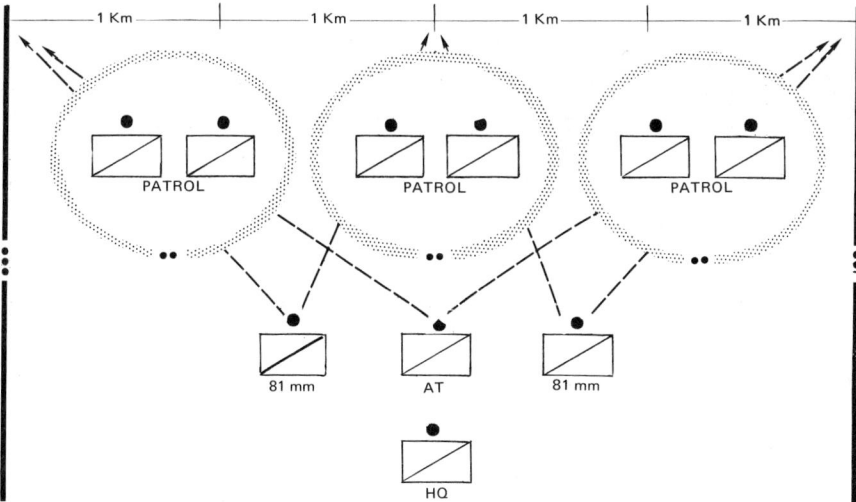

Figure 1.

COMMAND AND SUPPORT DETACHMENT (17 men, 4 vehicles)
   Command team (5 men, 1 vehicle)
      1 Lieutenant, 1 NCO, 2 radio operators, 1 driver
      1 light car

   Anti-tank squad (4 men, 1 vehicle)
      1 NCO, 2 men, 1 driver
      1 light car with trailer, 1 anti-tank missile launcher

   Mortar section (8 men, 2 vehicles)
      2 NCOs, 4 men, 2 drivers
      2 light trucks, 2 81-mm mortars

Mobile Commando Squadron Groups

The group of squadrons combines the action of six mobile commando platoons, deployed two echelons in depth to allow for withdrawal maneuver. These six platoons are commanded by a Major and his executive officer, a Captain. They are logistically supported by a command and service platoon whose structure is shown on the opposite page. The group of squadrons totals 327 men and 69 vehicles, and their field disposition is shown in Figure 2.

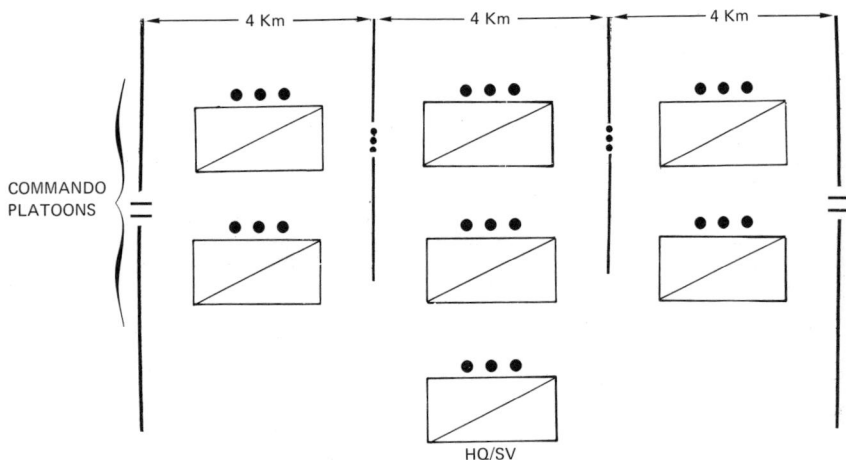

Figure 2.

It is worth noting that this contingent—of hardly conventional appearance—is clearly more economical than the usual triangular organization. The latter would lead to an average total expense (intervention troops included) of 130 men per kilometer, while the proposed organization costs only 55 men per kilometer.

Command and Service Platoon

COMMAND GROUP (25 men, 4 vehicles)
Command team (5 men, 1 vehicle)
    1 Major, 1 Lieutenant, 2 radio operators, 1 driver
    1 light car

Executive team (5 men, 1 vehicle)
    1 Captain, 1 NCO, 2 radio operators, 1 driver
    1 light car

Headquarters detachment (6 men, 1 vehicle)
    1 NCO, 2 radio operators, 2 clerks, 1 driver
    1 small truck

Security detachment (9 men, 1 vehicle)
    1 NCO 3 riflemen
    1 small truck

SERVICE GROUP (20 men, 5 vehicles)
Administrative detachment (4 men, 1 vehicle)
    1 Adjutant, 2 clerks, 1 driver
    1 light car

Motor pool detachment (4 men, 1 vehicle)
    1 NCO, 2 men, 1 driver
    1 small truck

Quartermaster detachment (8 men, 2 vehicles)
    2 NCOs, 6 men
    2 small trucks

Medical detachment (4 men, 1 vehicle)
    1 NCO, 2 aid men, 1 driver

MOBILE COMMANDO REGIMENT

Covering a front of 36 kilometers, the mobile commando regiment (2061 men) combines the action of three commando squadron groups with that of two anti-tank combat squadrons meant to oppose enemy armored thrusts. It also has a squadron of combat Engineers (200 men) responsible for destruction and obstruction as well as the possible missions of defending a locality. There is also a 300-man command and logistics squadron at the regimental level.

Each of the anti-tank combat squadrons is organized as follows:

4 COMBAT ANTI-TANK PLATOONS (50 men, 11 vehicles)
    5 anti-tank missile squads (20 men, 5 light cars)
    5 rifle squads (25 men, 5 light cars)
    1 command squad (5 men, 1 light car)

SUPPORT PLATOON (45 men, 6 81-mm mortars, 9 vehicles)

COMMAND AND LOGISTICS PLATOON (45 men, 9 vehicles)

The regimental field deployment is shown in Figure 3.

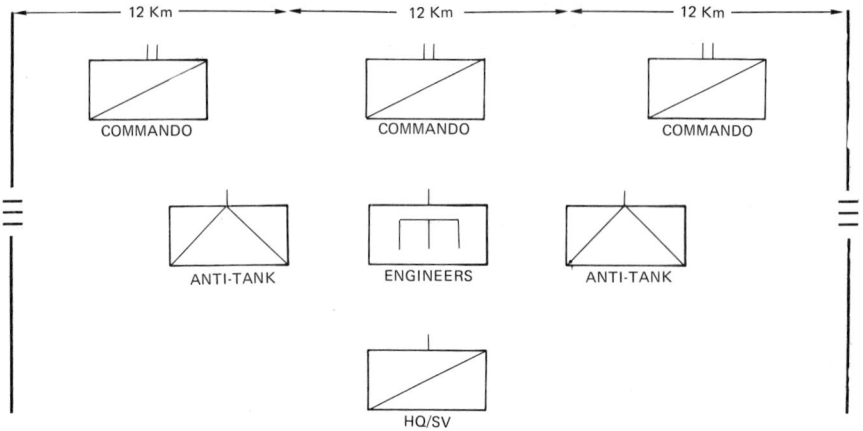

Figure 3.

Mobile Commando Division

The mobile commando division, destined to constitute the mobile curtain, includes:

5 mobile commando regiments 10,305

1 combat anti-tank regiment
   4 anti-tank combat squadrons 1,160
   1 tank squadron 200
   1 support squadron 200
   1 command and logistics squadron 300   1,860

1 command and logistics regiment 2,000
                                    Total 14,165

It covers a front of 100 kilometers as shown in Figure 4. Armament includes 370 anti-tank cannon along the front as well as 264 mortars. This is not a battle unit, but it can provide an elastic front which is both inexpensive and very efficient. The six divisions of mobile commandos are instructed and mobilized through a border region from a division by half-contingent.

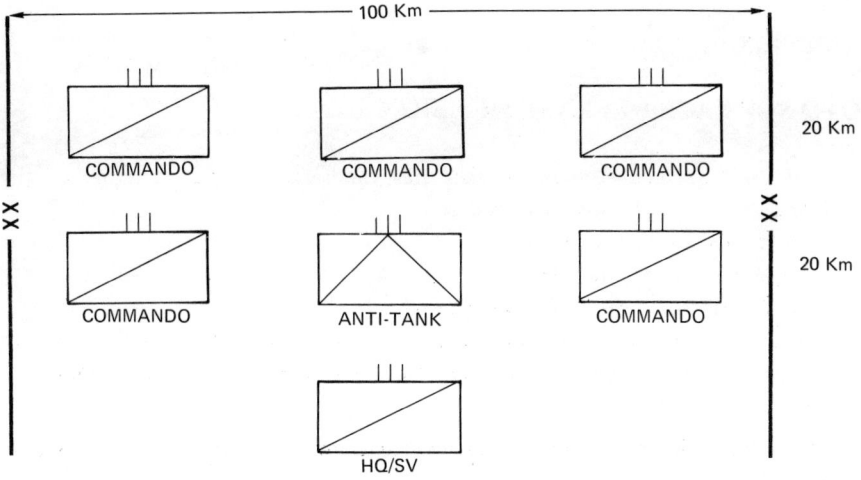

Figure 4.

APPENDIX III

OTD SURFACE DEFENSE DIVISION

The OTD *surface defense division* has the same general structure as the mobile commando division. It includes:
   a. 5 surface defense regiments
   b. 1 intervention regiment
   c. 1 command and logistics regiment

Because of the distances involved, it is completely motorized, based on civil-type vehicles, but with lighter armament than that of the mobile commando division.

The surface defense regiment has the same general structure as the mobile commando regiment:
   a. 3 battalions of surface defense troops, comprised of six defense platoons,
   b. 2 intervention companies
   c. 1 Infantry/Engineer company
   d. 1 command and service company.

The surface defense platoon (47 men, 10 vehicles) includes:
   a. 3 commando squads, each of which has
   b. 1 command and support group   5 men, 1 light car
         command team   4 men, 1 light car
         anti-tank team (rocket launcher)   4 men, 1 small truck
         mortar team (60-mm mortar)   4 men, 1 light car
         security team

The intervention platoon (50 men, 6 vehicles)
   a. 5 intervention squads, each of which has: 8 men, 1 driver, 1 small truck
   b. 1 command team (with recoilless rifle) 4 men, 1 driver, 1 car.

The intervention company (280 men)
   a. 4 combat platoons
   b. 1 support platoon (6 81-mm mortars)
   c. 1 command and logistics platoon.

The combat regiment
   a. 4 combat companies
   b. 1 anti-tank missile company
   c. 1 support company
   d. 1 command and logistics company.

When terrain responsibilities are being apportioned, a surface defense platoon will have about 100 km² to look after. A battalion covers 600 km², a regiment 1,800 km², a division 9,000 km², 54 divisions about 500,000 km².

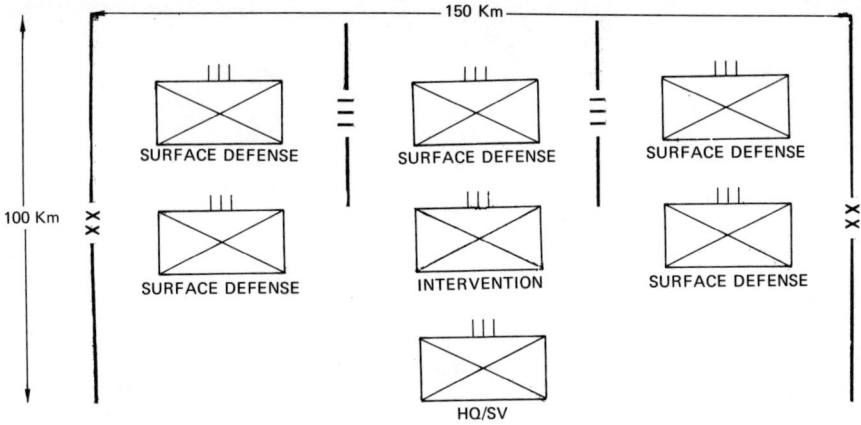

Figure 5.

Index

Algeria, 5
Algerian War, 6
Autonomous nuclear forces, 19-22
Armed forces
  future of, 72-74
Aviation, 30-32
  neutralization, 33-34

Biafra, 5

Chinese formula, 18
Clausewitz, 2
Conventional armament race, 17-18
Conventional blockade warfare, 64
Conventional warfare, 68-69
  against guerillas, 36-40
  analysis of, 27-32
  aviation, 30-32
  definition of, 26-27
  fait accompli, strategy of, 34-35
  fencing, 38-40
  firepower, 30
  forces, volume and quantity of, 28
  naval forces, 63
  operational theater, space of, 28-30
  persuasive strategy, 35-36
  strategic consequences, 34-36
Counter-offensive battle, 55-56
Credibility, 6

Deception tactics, 14
Destruction capacity, 6-7, 9-10
Deterrence, 18-19
  operational conditions, 52-53
  strategic conditions, 53-54
  tactical conditions, 51-54
  total nuclear war, 68

Egypt, 32
Escalation, 3, 8-10

Fait accompli, strategy, 34-35, 68
Fencing, 28-30
  guerilla warfare, 36-40
Fire power, 30
Flexible response doctrine, 9-10
Forward strategy, 10, 54
France, 6, 10
  autonomous nuclear buildup, 19-22

Germany, 19
Globalization, 23, 73
Great Britain, 6, 19
Guerilla warfare, 26-27
  fencing factor, 36-40
  strategic consequences, 39-40

ICBM, 14-15
Inflatable army, 71
Interception, 14-15
Intercontinental logistics, 64
Israel
  air power, 31, 32
Israeli-Egyptian War, 31

Kahn, Herman, 9

La Guerre Révolutionnaire (Beaufre),
  27
Level 0, 20-21, 69-70
Level 1, 20-22, 70
Level 2, 70
Level 3, 70
Limited war, 11
  characteristics of, 2-3

renaissance of, 2
total strategy, 2-3
Local mobilization, 55

Mass media, 5-6
Megadeath, 6-7
Military adventurism, 3
Military problems, 69-71
Military Strategy (Sokolowski), 9
MIRV, 14-15
Mobile commando division, 84
Mobile commando platoon, 81-82
Mobile commando regiment, 83-84
Mobile commando squadron groups,
   82-83
Mobile defense, 47
Mobile screen, 54-55
Mobilization, 72
Moral deterrence, 5
Motorized militia, 55
Multiple Independent Reentry
   Vehicles *see* MIRV
McNamara, Robert, 9, 48

Nation-States, 23
NATO, 10
Naval forces, 63-64
Navy, 59-61
News media
   warfare, role of, 4
No first use, 16
Non-spasmodic nuclear war, 16
Nuclear deterrence, 6
Nuclear strategy, 8

On Escalation (Kahn), 9
Operational theater, 28-30
Organized Territorial Defense units, 77
   conception and structure of, 78
   organization of, 79-80
OTD Mobile Defense Division, 81-84
OTD Surface Defense Division, 86-87

Penetration tactics, 14
Persuasive strategy, 35-36
Portugal, 5
Preemptive counterforce capacity, 7
Propaganda, 4-5

Reciprocal threat, 7-8
Rise to the extremes, 2, 3

SALT negotiations, 10, 15-17
   strategic consequences, 17-19
Satellites, 15, 20
Schmidt, Helmut, 10
Sea
   role in conflict, 61-63
Six-Day War, 6, 34
Sokolowski, 9, 15, 50
Soviet Union
   naval forces, 64
   nuclear escalation, 9
   SALT negotiations, 15-17
   tactical nuclear weapons, use of, 48-
      49
Spasm nuclear war *see* Total nuclear
   war
Spasm war, 16
Strategic nuclear deterrence
   naval forces, 63
   uncertainty and priority of tech-
      nique, 13-15
Strategic nuclear umbrella, 10
Submarines, 63
Suez Canal, 5, 33
Sufficiency, 8

Tactical atomic weapons, 69
   conditions for deterrent action, 51-54
   deterrent exploitation of, 49-51
   operational conditions, use of, 52
   psychological consequences, 50
   strategic conditions, use of, 53-54
   tactical conditions, 51-52

Tactical maneuver
  aerial forces and, 32-34
  guerilla warfare, 37-38
Tactical nuclear deterrence, 43-57
  counter-offensive battle, 55-56
  evolution, perspectives for, 56
  mobile screen, 54-55
  naval forces, 63-64
Tactical nuclear weapons 43-45
  characteristics of 44-45
  use of 45-49, 51
Threat, use of 18-19
Total nuclear war, 67-68
Total strategy
  characteristics of, 2-3
  constraints of, 3-10

United States
  nuclear escalation 9-10
  satellites, 15-17
  tactical nuclear weapons, use of, 47-48

Vietnam, 5, 31, 38

Warfare
  changing nature of, 1-2
  news media, role of, 4
  world opinion and, 5-6
  see also Limited warfare
Western Europe, 10
World opinion, 5-6